Transforming to
GROW

Profiles of Change
from the
Lehigh Valley

Phil Mitman
Richard A. Anderson
Caroll Neubauer
David Jaindl
Dr. Alice P. Gast
Dr. Christopher Bennick
Greg Butz
Maria Rodale
Dr. John Malloy
Dr. Elliot Sussman
Tony Iannelli
Gov. Tom Ridge

Written by
Thomas A. Malm

BRAINWORKS BOOKS
Philadelphia, Pennsylvania

BRAINWORKS BOOKS
The Imprint of T.A. Malm & Associates

Thomas Allen Malm is available for private consulting, business seminars, strategic planning retreats and public speaking engagements. Write info@tamalm.com for information. For quantity discounts for use in education and training programs, special promotions and sales premiums contact books@tamalm.com.

*Attention Booksellers: Contact books@tamalm.com for
stocking programs and special author appearances.*

T.A. Malm & Associates
Quakertown, Pennsylvania

*Special thanks to the great leaders
who told me their stories.*

Contents

Author's Note

Faith Is Restored

In the beginning of 2009, *Valley Social Magazine* asked me to write a series of articles profiling the leading CEO's of Pennsylvania's Lehigh Valley. Being deeply interested in the transformational strategic planning process and best practices in organizational leadership, it was a wonderful opportunity to "pick the brains" of the key leaders that drive the companies in what is among the most successful regional economies in the US. This is the first modern generation to lead at a time when the area's most significant industry wasn't steel. The leaders of this generation, naturally, had to create their own opportunities through change and innovation. For the survival of their institutions, they needed to join arms with a community spirit to advance the quality of life, the energy of the workforce and the foundations of the infrastructure. As such, the profiles of these individuals meld with the vitality of the community to exhibit the value of the "regional approach" that, if worked in every area of the country, could defend and strengthen the economy of America.

The stories that follow are more inspiring than they are sexy. As they came together I began to see systematic approaches that reflected vision and ideals that might seem old-fashioned on Wall Street. There was no question that these leaders were all aggressive market competitors. But their missions are the kind that never let them lose sight of the fact that success demands focus beyond the current month's end or the next quarter's profit posting. At their core, these leaders all know how business can run at its best, how employees can be most excellent and how dependent upon their competence are the families and other businesses in the community.

I also included a story from my conversation with former Governor Tom Ridge as he discussed the challenges of change when he was called upon to create the Department of Homeland Security. As tasks go, his experience in binding the various cultures within the political landscape of Washington, DC is as instructional as it is entertaining. Organizationally, it is possible that no one has met such an enormous challenge with such high odds for failure.

If there is good news for America it comes in the example of solid ethics, genuine innovation and clear vision when much of the nation seems confused. Since the 1980's the standards for measuring the nation's financial health shifted from a production measurement to purely financial results determined by quarterly profit outcomes that drive the stock market ticker. Business strategist and consultant Lewis Fein described what he called "The MBA Syndrome" in the 1980's, warning that colleges were churning a multitude of graduates with MBAs into the workforce with the single intent of making as much money as fast as they could with the least amount of risk. The incentives were great and the methods for tracking progress were malleable. What that would produce was not very surprising.

A string of crimes accounted for nearly half of the most significant brands to disappear in the last quarter-century. The DotCom boom and crash, the unsustainable and difficult to monitor derivative products of Wall Street and the sub-prime lending mentality that pushed untenable "bottom-line" profits were not much less criminal than the outright theft of Bernie Madoff. The end result in every case was ruined lives.

It is troubling to me that as a nation we are fixated by Donald Trump's TV Show that in no way exemplifies the best proven practices of business management, organizational leadership and sustainable enterprise. We need more examples of strong businesses that can see patiently past the next commercial break to find something sustainable. We need more leaders that capitalize on the value of learning that comes from making mistakes. It isn't hard to imagine that if the Trump persona we see on television ran 3M, some poor scientist would be jobless and the company would miss the entire Post It Note industry born from error. We need different role models. What is most important in business and what is most important about community are the same. People of character. People of vision. People on a mission. Good people.

These pages share the stories of heroes too reluctant to accept their laurels. Their companies operate with long-term vision and with missions to build, create and produce values for customers, their employee families and the community. The companies are different. Their leaders are very different from each other. Yet, they all share some common characteristics that can return America to the strength it had in better times if all business leaders and shareholders followed their standards. They have what will help to make America greater.

Heroes. We usually assign that word to warriors and athletes for various exploits that transcend man's natural abilities and character. The USA is a nation that may have gotten comfortable with a status quo that continues to erode its status. In a country in which free enterprise is the foundation of prosperity the real patriots and soldiers are those willing to see the bigger picture and protect the safety and stability of their associates and employees, their stakeholders, their customers, their communities and – most importantly - the purest code of business ethics. This book features people whose skills can transfer to the leadership of any company or organization. They are people who see the stewarding of their organizations onto the next generation as a primary responsibility. America needs more of these kinds of leaders in order to reclaim territory in global battlefield.

A wise person will enjoy the stories being told on a level deeper than the entertaining anecdotes. They will see examples against which they can examine their own strengths and weaknesses. They will reflect and compare – not just the actions and methods – but the deeper attributes of vision, ethics, hard work, respect, character and community. There is a connectedness that each company has with the region that participates to make it stronger and more vital. They build businesses for reasons greater than building wealth. Hopefully this idea will touch everyone that reads their stories. Hopefully they will spark a new paradigm to influence all companies – public and private, big and small.

The Lehigh Valley is American business at its best. It is a place where transformation is the operative word and community is the common cause. It is a place where jobs, prosperity, quality of life and legacy are the outcomes of vision, mission, strategy and conscience. To be sure, I won't be hawking this book through any infomercial with promises it will change your life. There isn't much chance you're going to get rich tomorrow by reading this. However, there is every chance that if you have a modest amount of the wisdom, vision and character of these leaders you can be on your way to creating a legacy. You can put your faith in that.

Phil Mitman

Lehigh Valley Economic Development Corporation

There's a bust of a Native American Chief that sits on one corner of Phil Mitman's desk. There are other artifacts that decorate the walls of his office to suggest that his interest in the original Americans is more than casual. Since his early days as a Boy Scout, Mitman says the philosophy of the first inhabitants of North America regarding their responsibility to the land has made a great impression on him. "They believed we don't own the land. We're its caretakers. Our responsibility is to leave things better than we found them."

When he speaks of his role as the Chief Executive Officer of the Lehigh Valley Economic Development Corporation, you realize quickly that Phil Mitman is the ideal caretaker. As he tells it, he grew up in the

"It really is about sticking to the Strategic Plan every day . . ."

Lehigh Valley, worked in his well-established family business (Bixler's Jewelers), and as a kid the value and importance of service was engrained in him. He learned early that customer service and meeting the needs of the people in the community were the keys to prosperity and success. He seems keenly

12

aware that with his family's connectedness to the community comes the responsibility to serve it. That's what led him to serve as Easton's Mayor. It's what appealed to him about the Lehigh Valley Economic Development Corporation. "I'm very honored to have this work because I absolutely love it. The vision of the [founding] leaders - the regional approach - is in every bone of my body."

The Lehigh Valley Economic Development Corporation was born from the vision of fifteen of the most influential community leaders of the 1990's. The original Articles of Incorporation define the purpose of the nonprofit simply and with no ambiguity. "To develop and affect a program to achieve and sustain balanced job growth in the Lehigh Valley." As a filter for all of the LVEDC's activities, this statement has evolved into a vision for the organization to be the region's driving force for economic development. Taking on the mission to lead the Lehigh Valley to continued prosperity, today the investor-based development corporation includes over two-hundred-seventy-five investor/members. The LVEDC engages leadership from the area's major public and private-owned corporations, two counties and their elected and appointed officers, three significant cities and their representatives, and a range of other community organizations and entities. The leaders of these entities combine to make up the Board of Directors and a range of committees that see to the work of the LVEDC.

To a casual observer of human nature, such a mix of personalities, individual interests, and politics could be the formula for gridlock, stagnation, and an impossible situation for the LVEDC's CEO. However, Mitman smiles while explaining that the organization works primarily *because* of the range of influence and input from the area's power players. "It actually is quite easy and very collaborative. I have never seen a more dedicated organization of people coming together to make things happen."

The collaborative spirit of the LVEDC was among the first impressions he had of the organization when he first took its reigns. "I was very positively surprised about a number of things. The leaders on the board, the officers and the executive committee were, and are, so totally committed to this Lehigh Valley regional approach to economic development and partnerships." Mitman says this commitment can be tangibly measured in the thousands of volunteer hours that are given by the member companies and particularly in the thousands of volunteer hours that are given by their leaders. In his earliest days as the LVEDC's CEO he was also surprised to discover an impressively high level of professionalism, quality, and dedication in the staff. "As a mayor, I was asked to serve on the executive committee. Of the four years and forty-eight meetings, I probably missed two. So I knew quite a bit of what went on here, and yet, I didn't know what all of the staff did. The staff was much more knowledgeable and professional than I ever knew."

According to the CEO, the talent of the professional staff drives the work that the organization gets done. He sees his role as creating the opportunities for them to succeed. "I do what I can to empower our professional staff here. They are terrific. There are young professionals. There are some older people like myself. I do everything to empower them because it's all about LVEDC continuing, doing a fantastic job, and being one of the best economic development organizations in Pennsylvania."

Perhaps the quality and work of the staff had been overshadowed by a period when press coverage for the Lehigh Valley Economic Development Committee was less than flattering. Strong criticism in the media eroded its credibility. "You might recall that starting in 2002 or so there were articles in all the papers about how LVEDC was a closed community - about how they didn't share their financials and all that. When I went in for the CEO interviews, [there had been] six years of articles that said it was a closed organization. And we're not. The original visionaries did not envision it as a closed community." Mitman says that in his first year it was really important to go out and rebuild the trust and the relationships all over the Lehigh Valley. He met individually with the LVEDC members, with elected officials and appointed officers. He summarizes his mission in a single word. "Trust. In my opinion, and the opinion of some in the community, LVEDC lost trust within the community."

Perhaps the need for someone who could rebuild relationships was why he was the ideal candidate to oversee the LVEDC. His private business and public service resume made him a well-known personality whose ethics and integrity had been exhibited on the public stage. He was a local leader whose genuine interest in the economic vitality of the region came with established credibility. "I was in private business, was an elected official, and helped to run some not-for-profits and things like that. The whole family-connectedness around the Lehigh Valley was very helpful and I hope that's one of the reasons they chose me to help LVEDC. I could call any of the elected officials at any time. I could go to see them. They knew who I was, and hopefully, knew my past and the best integrity I could bring to the job . . . I found in all of my discussions – and I was doing more listening than talking – that the private companies I met with, the not-for-profits I met with, the elected officials and appointed officials all wanted LVEDC to succeed . . . I listened to their needs. And the trust came back. Going through the search process with eighty other applicants, and the interview processes, and the written thing I had to go through with the committee, it was clear that they wanted a more open person. They wanted a Lehigh Valley person, as it turns out. That was very important because the goal has always been from the [founding] visionaries, through today, to be the best model in Pennsylvania of regionalism, collaboration, and partnership." He says he strives to be frank, open, and honest regardless of the sensitivity of an issue. "So if you ask me any question I'll do the very best I can to answer it. If it's a 'yes,' here's why. If it's a 'no,' here's why. But I won't skirt the issue."

Today, it would be impossible to not know what the LVEDC does, where its priorities lie, and how they will take action. The LVEDC is open regarding money and how it is spent. Following the best practices of the most stable companies and organizations in the world, they have dedicated over a year of energy and thousands of professional and volunteer man-hours to create a comprehensive five-year Strategic Plan. As CEO, Mitman considers himself just one leader among many. His primary role is to execute the formal five-year Strategic Plan that he describes as being ushered forward by three men in the organization – Bill Michalerya, Don Bernhard, and Robert Episcopo. These men and the LVEDC staff worked for fourteen months on a plan that includes the talents and input from one-hundred-twenty-five other people. It includes the vision and ideas from the elected officials, the legislators and their appointed officers, and LVEDC board members. Through this collaboration, they have identified six industry clusters that are targeted for retention, attraction and expansion. The LVEDC's plan has identified and detailed fifteen specific strategic actions, programs, and projects that will receive the focus and effort necessary to deliver on the organization's promise to its investors and the community. All of this is summarized in five strategic priorities that distill down to powerful words of action: cultivate, advance, intensify, boost, and create.

The goals are specific. The measure of success or failure is critically defined through projected outcomes. There's a whole lot more to it, ranging from research and demographic studies, site location services, financing support, marketing projects, green initiatives, recycling, women and minority business development, foreign trade, and the creation of expansion and innovation opportunities. The ambitions for the region are the product of unbridled imaginations, filtered through realistic vision, and applied in ways that address the ultimate needs of the region. To be sure, there are no secrets about any of it. The

17

mission is clear. "This is about economic development going forward."

The Lehigh Valley Economic Development Corporation is the only entity paid to market the Lehigh Valley to attract companies and to have companies expand here. While the LVEDC actively contacts prospective companies to see if they would like to come here, most of the companies come here because of professional site selectors. "Site selectors are hired by companies. A company will say, 'Find us a site that meets these criteria.' They go to the internet. The site selector will go to websites designed to be helpful in narrowing their search. The site selector will be able to find the current inventory of available buildings and all kinds of other information for almost every location in America. As a key tool for attracting new business, the LVEDC has recently committed to a significant upgrading and redesign of the website with a Lehigh Valley company. "I said when I first got here, 'We're going to 'Buy Lehigh Valley.' If we are given the opportunity to showcase the Lehigh Valley to the entrepreneurs and the businesses looking to expand or come here, they like the fact that we are very connected."

Mitman says he has been told by businesses that have landed here, instead of somewhere else, that there are a several key reasons. One reason has been the business climate in Pennsylvania supported by the Ridge and Rendell administrations. "Pennsylvania has been much more aggressive under the Rendell administration and the legislators to make it business-friendly and give incentive money to have you come here. Workforce money for your training of your company." The not-for-profit economic development corporation is also well-connected in other areas of influence that might help a prospective company move or expand in the Lehigh Valley. "Here at LVEDC, any of us can make a call to [U.S. Congressman] Charlie Dent, Senator Casey or Senator Specter and their offices and get attention. Because those elected officials and the private sector know that we want to create quality jobs, we all work together so [the companies we attract] can count on their resources coming together. The regionalism approach is working." There's an element of local pride that Mitman exposes as he says that high among the elements that make the Lehigh Valley an attractive region for growth and expansion is its people. "The workforce – [the companies that have grown in the Lehigh Valley] knew they could get a workforce that was willing to work and had a good work ethic."

Today the Lehigh Valley is very attractive to businesses. But the purpose of a Strategic Plan is to take a long range view and honestly assess the prospects for continued prosperity. The value of looking with strategic objectivity toward the future is that it naturally promotes the actions that ensure sustained prosperity. Among the action items that Mitman discusses that will be vital to making the Lehigh Valley economically successful in the future is "to be encouraging the young professionals, the young talent, to stay here." Working with the colleges and organizations dedicated to the young professional, the LVEDC has created a task force that stays "absolutely focused" on keeping young talent in the region. "I had [met] with a company recently that said, 'We have three-hundred baby-boomers retiring in the next five years. We're going to have three-hundred positions opened in this very engineering-based category. Where are we going to get those? We're going to need to recruit them . . . We need the young professionals to stay here.' What we're doing here at LVEDC - with the Chamber and others - is to attract those companies that will be able to pay better wages for the young professionals here. Young professionals aren't always saying, 'Where are the best jobs?' They're asking, 'Where do I want to live,' then [they'll] look for the job."

Among the initiatives of the LVEDC is to create a community that offers an attractive quality-of-life to match its attractive economic opportunities. The energy devoted to opportunities for young professionals is equaled by the LVEDC's focus on creating the environment to promote success in other growing sectors of the community. Women and minority businesses are actively encouraged through specific actions defined in the Strategic Plan. "The LVEDC was asked by the Mayor of Allentown, Ed Pawlowski and the Allentown Economic Development Corporation, to take over the minority women-owned business [initiative] which they had started there. They said, 'Let's take it across the Lehigh Valley.' So we took over and call it the Office of Minority and Women Owned Business. We have a full-time director who works on promoting the best opportunities for Latino, African-American, and other minority enterprises, as well as encouraging women-owned businesses."

Under Mitman's guidance, the LVDC has strived to make the organization work with efficiency and a keen sense of fiduciary responsibility. He's aligned the organization and size of the professional staff to be in accord with the LVEDC's objectives. "We talk a lot about, 'What is the value that we can bring to our investors, the members?" He speaks quite openly about the state of financial affairs. "Regardless of the fact that our revenues are down $720 thousand, regardless of any other issues, we are totally dedicated to implementing our five strategic priorities. We came out with a new financing brochure. We have the Strategic Plan. And for the first time in LVEDC's history, we have dipped into the reserve contingency fund for some of '09 expenses that we can't meet on revenues.

"For 2010 we've balanced the budget by dipping in, because that's what it is for. We're using a total of $220 thousand from our reserve fund – and that's a very good thing. We're very fortunate for those [original] leaders. When the hotel tax started, they socked away $1 million and said, 'We're going to need that." Mitman says that any well run business keeps reserves to ensure its survival though tough times. "And if this isn't a 'rainy day,' I don't know what is." Revenues may be down, but the energy and resources of the LVEDC are at work, prudently invested to keep the Lehigh Valley ahead of the recovery curve. While the staff has been reduced in some areas, it has grown in others that will lead to a sustainable growth environment.

"I and other leaders for LVEDC knew we needed to recruit some other professionals. So we recruited John Kingsley, to be our Vice President of Finance, and he is doing a phenomenal job with helping businesses all over the region to finance their projects, finance their businesses, expand their businesses, help grow jobs. The other person we recruited was Bob Bilheimer, and he is the Vice President of Fund Development and Investor Relations. He has brought in thirty-five new members since he has been here in March. We were losing membership before."

Along with a quality work force and a pro-business political climate, businesses considering the Lehigh Valley are able to see that the overall quality of the region is constantly improving. "One of the things we work on at the LVEDC is to work on the urban cores. Having been a mayor, I know full well that the health of the cities really has a heck of a lot to do with the health of the entire region. So we want the communities, the downtowns and so forth, to be cleaner and safer. And it's difficult, it's a challenge. But we keep at that day-in and day-out here at LVEDC. So they like that. And then they see that the museums, the new restaurants that have come in the last five to ten years - and they continue to open. The families seem to be accepting of us unless they need the multi-million population cities. We might lose some deals to the South or the West, and it might be because the CEO and his family doesn't want to be in the East or something. But we get our fair share. It's just a very friendly place to come in."

With a committed investor group, the leadership talent from most of the area's major private and public entities, and an upgraded and empowered professional staff, the LVEDC seems to be making its mark. By many reports the Lehigh Valley is among the fastest growing Market Statistical Areas in the Northeast. To Mitman, that's the ultimate report card for the value of the LVEDC today and moving forward. And forward is where he is focused. "We see very positive trends on the recovery side for the Lehigh Valley. We're certainly focusing on the [six] diverse industry cluster groups. We're going to very much focus on, not the big businesses, but the medium and small. It's mostly small businesses that grow. We're very pleased that Olympus is here, but that probably not too many of those are going to start moving any time soon. It really is about sticking to the Strategic Plan every day, with the professional staff we have, the board, the officers, and all the partners we have in The Valley, because they created the Strategic Plan. My job is to help carry it out. I stay low-key most of the time, want to help be an empowering leader to the best of my ability, and we have a very bright future."

Since 1995, the year the LVEDC was chartered, the area has seen new jobs grow at twice the rate of Pennsylvania. The area has seen world-class recognition and award-winning achievement from its companies. The urban cores are being revitalized. But the objectives of the LVEDC are all based upon a vision for the future. "I want to say that no matter who is the next Governor, we want to make sure going forward that we are well noticed in the Lehigh Valley. So we are going to be more unified than ever with our leadership, not just at LVEDC, but around The Valley. We're working with many kinds of organizations partnering to make sure the Lehigh Valley is noticed in the next administration, because we are really good here. We're a generator of jobs. We have a quality-of-life here. We're a model, not only for Pennsylvania, but particularly with the Brownfield site and the urban core work, we're really a model for the country."

A model for the country. The area is growing and vital. Phil Mitman, through his genuine call to service, is the conduit for this achievement. Perhaps his most important skill is in coordinating the multitude of forces - the local municipalities, the Federal, State and County government entities, the global corporations operating in the region, and the regionally-based and local businesses. With the plan they have created in hand, the future for the Lehigh Valley is thoughtfully charted for upward progress.

He is the Chief Executive Officer, indeed. But for the Lehigh Valley Economic Development Corporation, CEO could also mean the Caretaker of Economic Opportunity. Like the Native American Chief whose bust sits on his desk, Phil Mitman understands and respects the need for sustainability in his environment. As such, he will surely leave things in the Lehigh Valley better than he found them.

Richard A. Anderson

St. Luke's Hospital and Health Network

Author's note: This story was written before any national healthcare programs were passed by Congress.

St. Luke's Hospital & Health Network's Chief Executive Officer, Richard A. Anderson uses straight-forward language. There is no need for carefully constructed sound-bites or well-spun talking points because the axiom "actions speak louder than words" has no better example.   What has been achieved under his direction tells an eloquent story of the man and the people he leads. When speaking about the vast complexities of healthcare, the foundation of successful business management, and the promise of the Lehigh Valley, he is reflective, introspective,

"Change is constant. If you think there's status quo, then you're probably in the wrong seat . . . If you're too compulsive, it'll eat you alive."

and contemplative. "I love what I'm doing. I enjoy coming to work every day. I wouldn't say it's fun. I wouldn't want to be flip about it because caring for people is serious business. But I do have a lot of fun."

There was a time in his career, before joining St. Luke's, when Anderson was the youngest CEO of a health facility in the State. Coming to St. Luke's in 1985, he is now the longest-tenured Chief Executive of a healthcare network in Pennsylvania. "This is a business not for the faint of heart. Change is constant. If you think there's status quo, then you're probably in the wrong seat . . . If you're too compulsive, it'll eat you alive. As Darwin said, 'It's not the strongest who survive, but the ones who can change most quickly.' Positive change has come under Anderson's leadership, but he defuses any suggestion that he brought any special magic to the hospital. "I think what I found here were really good people who wanted to do the right thing. I just built on that. I built on the culture that was here."

There are few examples where Darwinian business theory is demonstrated as clearly as healthcare. Success can be influenced by the constantly changing culture of the country, public opinion, political pressures, financial realities, intense competition, and the needs of the community. It demands adaptable leadership. According to the book, *Best Practices in Leadership Development and Organizational Change* written by Louis Carter, David Ulrich, and Marshall Goldsmith, Anderson introduced St. Luke's to the concept of transforming managers into leaders. "That's as applicable today as it was then. Any transformational manager wants to leave the organization better than they found it. When I say 'transformational leader,' I'm not talking about me. It isn't about me. It's about a team of individuals.

"I couldn't have framed this then, what I'm about to tell you now. But when I talk to young people and individuals who are starting out, I tell them it's really important what they get in school. Education and experience are very important. But at the end of the day, whatever you do - whether you're a banker, a stock broker, a writer, an administrator, a CEO – it all comes down to your relationships with people and how you treat them." Working with people, and creating a culture that respects and acknowledges their contributions is important. Beneath such a simple principle is a much more complicated art of drawing the best from people through their personal quirks and individual human qualities. "We're all passionate - every one of us. You go to work and interact with all the other passionate people. But it's how you manage all that passion. Some of us are immature, we're petty. I know I've had my days. But it's learning how to put it in the right balance. Tell me who has not really been fair to you over the last five years, or who treated you kind of crappy. You'd remember. You might be past it, but you'd remember. When the people who treated you well say, 'Hey, could you do me a favor?' you'd say, 'Sure, what can I do for you.' If the person who didn't treat you well called, you'd say, 'Well, I'm kind of busy today.' What goes around comes around."

Don't be mistaken, the idea that treating people well and cultivating good relationships are the keys to success does not mean St. Luke's culture is founded on happy faces and gentle kindnesses between employees. To be clear, Anderson acknowledges the challenges of survival and growth don't fit neatly into such one-dimensional platitudes. "I don't want to come off as some goodie-two-shoes. I'm as fierce a competitor as you'll find. I can be a pretty tough coach if there's something to get done in a certain way. I can be like a Bill Belichick or a Bill Parcells, who's out there really holding people's feet to the fire." St. Luke's CEO sees conflict, and the energy it can create to promote improvement, as a vital element of the hospital's results-driven environment. "You can't expect to have a group of Stepford Wives or Stepford Husbands around always agreeing to everything you're saying all the time, or the organization gets stale and it won't grow. So you need some conflict. Change occurs because there are many people sharing vision and working together – not always in harmony. I do keep the cultural keys. I'm, at times, the policemen on how people get treated. I do pay attention to those kinds of things . . . Most of the time people will do the right thing. I tell people it's not important to be right. It's important to do the right thing. And that's hard sometimes.

"Because we provide health services and we don't make widgets, fenders, or computer chips, we literally deal with peoples lives every day. We have a responsibility to each and every employee we have, to give them a living wage and good benefits so they can take care of their family. We have all of the patients who come in, and the community depends on us." He considers everyone who walks in as an opportunity to make a positive contribution to a life, a family, a community. He admits it doesn't always happen. People sometimes are not at their best. "When people come in, you have a responsibility to try to do what you can and fulfill their expectations – and sometimes you don't do that."

St. Luke's was initially chartered to serve the workers at the Steel Foundries in Bethlehem. Before St. Luke's, injured workers would be put on the train to be treated in Philadelphia. Many of the seriously injured did not survive the trip, creating a critical community need. The recent growth and success of the hospital has expanded its ability to expand the original community-service vision upon which the hospital was founded. Assessing the needs of the area in the 1990s, St. Luke's found a lot of the kids needed dental care, mental health or just some basic primary care. "So we put together a plan and started to work with all the different community agencies. It was called – and still is – The Bethlehem Partnership for Healthy Community. Donors helped us buy some health and dental vans. Together with our partners, we provide the know-how. But, the way the work gets done is by using all of the community agencies to help provide the service work - the school districts, Turning Point, and some of the other organizations that help people who don't have the same access to healthcare that maybe you do and I do. It's worked out well. We've served thousands and thousands of children and adults."

Looking backward, Anderson describes how, two-and-a-half decades ago, St. Luke's might not have been fit enough to flourish in the competitive environment that was coming. It wasn't that they had substandard talent and skills, provided inferior services, or were burdened with a poor reputation for patient care. What he discovered when he first arrived was a fundamentally sound culture. Yet, there was an issue with its leadership. "It was a small hospital, in the sense of how things were structured. Managerially, the people had what I'd call an organizational inferiority complex." He sensed that the people within St. Luke's had deep concerns. "Everybody was afraid the next shoe would drop - that they weren't going to be around or that they weren't going to have a job, or that our doctors or nurses weren't as good as the next organization. None of that was true."

This attitude Anderson didn't initially understand. "In my early days, I went down to the Moravian Church and was walking around the graveyard. I remember all of the tombstones were flat. I asked the local preacher at the time, 'Why are they all flat?' He explained it was because 'Everybody in the eyes of The Lord is equal." The principle that all are equal may have manifested into accepting that all should be equal. In the culture he found at St. Luke's, excellence was quietly executed. The competitors were doing a better job of promoting themselves. "I would hear the other guys were just bragging about what they could do – and I said, 'they're not better than we are. [The first step toward transforming the culture came from] just reminding everybody of all the qualities that were here, and of all the good that they had done, and of all the talented individuals that were employed here - being a cheerleader." The core problems he found at St. Luke's were insular.

By bringing a much needed competitive drive to St. Luke's, Anderson helped the organization to see itself differently. In twenty-five years, this new drive and confidence grew St. Luke's from a single hospital to the largest geographically distributed healthcare network on its landscape. St. Luke's today includes over one-hundred-fifty network facilities that span sixty-three miles from north to south and serve communities in eight counties. The four hospitals in the network admit more than 44,000 patients each year who are cared for by 1,200 physicians, more than 7,000 employees, and 1,200 volunteers. "This organization, with help from a lot of people, has regularly reinvented itself. Twenty years ago we maybe had a seventeen percent marketshare. We're up to thirty-five, thirty-six percent marketshare. That's how we measure one kind of success. I've no doubt that in five or six years we'll be up to forty percent of the marketshare." He is clear that's not his ultimate test of achievement. For him, it's having a community which recognizes that if they have a health issue, the first place to turn for treatment is St. Luke's. "If you walk down the hall in a mall and you said to somebody, 'I've got a medical condition. Where should I go for my healthcare?' You go to St. Luke's. Why? 'Because those people really care about what they do.' To me, that means more than the marketshare. That's a real source of pride for me. That's my way of saying it's a great, great organization."

The "great organization" isn't just covering more geographic territory and enjoying an increase in beds. He's overseen an operation that has received accreditation for Pennsylvania's first new Level I trauma center in more than fourteen years. St. Luke's is a national leader in Robotic Surgery, initiating the nation's first "surgical guarantee" program for patients undergoing robotic prostatectomy or minimally invasive reconstructive surgery for pelvic prolapse. A $125 million investment in the Allentown Campus produced a 104% increase of admissions since the former Allentown Osteopathic Medical Center joined St. Luke's in 1997. A dozen years ago, St. Luke's forged a strategic partnership with the University of Pennsylvania Health System. St. Luke's hosts the first Northeastern Pennsylvania clinical campus for Temple University's School of Medicine, providing clinical rotations for third and fourth years students. Medical education programs have expanded to include one-hundred-fifty-two resident/fellowship positions in seventeen accredited programs. St. Luke's is one of only four-hundred members of the Council of Teaching Hospitals. And the network recently announced plans to initiate the region's first medical school program in partnership with Temple University to meet the looming physician shortage. Thirty students will be accepted into the inaugural class of Medical School of Temple University/St. Luke's Hospital & Health Network beginning in August 2011. Special consideration for enrollment will be given to pre-med students from Lehigh University, Moravian College and Muhlenberg College who have achieved academic excellence and are currently enrolled in the "Early Assurance" program through St. Luke's and Temple. It is anticipated that other area colleges and universities also will participate.

"This announcement is significant in that this is the first medical school program in the Greater Lehigh Valley combining basic science courses and clinical rotations," said Anderson. "Tomorrow's doctors will not only train here, but actually will earn their medical degrees here upon successful completion of a competitive four-year program. Local students in good academic standing will be afforded the chance to get their medical degree while training in their own community."

"I am proud of St. Luke's proven track record in partnering with other organizations, such as Temple," says Mr. Anderson. "We not only have the resources and the organizational talent to complete successfully this endeavor with Temple, but our ability to form win-win, mutually respectful partnerships helps, in part, to control health care costs and ensures our community and our patients are well served both now and in the future."

Today, St. Luke's Hospital & Health Network is regarded world-wide as a premiere healthcare organization. It has been awarded thirty national awards for clinical excellence in the last eleven years. Twice, it has been recognized as a 100 Top Hospital in the United States. Several clinical services have been listed in the *U.S. News and World Report's* annual "America's Best Hospitals" edition. On multiple occasions, St. Luke's has been named as one of the "Best Places to Work on Pennsylvania." Anderson puts credit for the hospital's reputation where it belongs. "Our most important assets are our employees, because, together with our physicians, they're the ones who make it happen. The fact that several times we were recognized as one of the 100 Top Hospitals in the country: That's pretty special. You look and you see that you've put yourself in with the Cleveland Clinic, The Mayo Clinic – and we're the only healthcare organization in The Valley to get that kind of recognition."

Being ranked among the 100 Top Hospitals in America doesn't happen every year. "I think it makes it sweeter that you don't get it every year. There're five-thousand hospitals in the country. When you're one of the top one-hundred that means there's good care for the people. That means there's good management, there's good leadership." Not being recognized each year does not suggest any backsliding in the quality of his network's healthcare delivery. It's just a reality that comes with chasing excellence in the medical services industry. "Everybody's getting better and that's great for patients."

St. Luke's has been a leader in its quality improvement and patient safety efforts since early 2000 when they became one of only 250 hospitals which volunteered to participate in the National Hospital Quality Improvement Demonstration (HQID) Project sponsored by Medicare and Premier. The purpose of the HQID project is to identify whether financial incentives improve quality of care. Four years of HQID data demonstrates that the 250 hospitals participating in the HQID are performing much better than hospitals nationally in the 30 evidence-based clinical quality measures that are collected in this project. Participation also gave hospitals an opportunity to shape policy and decision-making at the federal level.

The HQID program helps monitor St. Luke's quality against the best. For example, St. Luke's scored in the ninety-fourth percentile in heart attack treatment when they started in program. They were in the top decile. "A year later, we're at ninety-fifth [percentile] but so are probably eighty percent of the hospitals [in the program]. In other words, we got better, but guess what? So did they. They got a lot better." Today, St. Luke's scores 99.4% for heart attack patient treatment and care, but falls in the second tier of the group's top performers. "And we're so much better [than we were when we started the program]. We're doing that and we're doing this. But yes, everyone else got so much better. They're copying us, we're copying them."

He explains that the difference between their current 99.4% and a 99.9% score was not due to the actual care patients received. He says that the ultimate result of the project is a sort of "cookbook" that defines specific steps in patient care. In the program, scores are based on documented actions. The aspirin that a seasoned physician might give without a second thought in the most routine and universally understood scenario has to be recorded on the chart to be scored in the program. "You don't document it, you weren't doing it. We were doing it, but we weren't always documenting it."

Standardizing the best practices in patient treatment is an initiative he supports. "That's what the government is going to do. The politicians aren't doing it. The bureaucrats are doing it. And everybody is going to take advantage of it. It's like when you go to an Old Navy store, you're going to get the same material, the same sewing, the same pattern, the same this and the same that. When you go to a lot of hospitals now, you're going to get the same care. Is that bad? No, I don't think so. That's good. It's more objective and less subjective." Such a movement toward pedantic processes in healthcare might not be an easy concept for experienced healthcare professionals to accept. "Some of the older doctors will say, 'That's no way to take care of a patient.' But it works. Infections are down, lengths of stay are down. Morbidity is down. More importantly, mortality is down."

In America, healthcare has becomes a key political topic from the kitchen table, to the office water cooler, to the Capitol Building. Anderson believes the best way St. Luke's can address the crisis in healthcare is to focus on the things that can be controlled. Over the next five years he says, "We need to pay attention to patient safety. Safety, quality and keeping our costs down - those three things. Hospitals can be dangerous places. So you want to make sure the organization is paying attention to patient safety and paying attention to quality." The current activities in Washington regarding the healthcare of the nation evoke the opinion of an experienced pragmatist.

"He [President Obama] is not going to get it passed the way he thinks. He's not going to be able to pay for it. He'll take that money right out of the hides of the hospitals and the doctors. Everybody thinks doctors are wealthy and millionaires – they're not. All these young people come out of medical school and they've got $180 thousand in debts. They're making less than $100 thousand per year as they complete their residencies. And hospitals – some of them are struggling. Some hospitals have margins less than two percent a year. Fortunately, we do a little better than that. We're a big business, but when you make a margin that's less than two percent - most businesses can't survive very long on less than two percent. So, he's going to take it out of the hides of the doctors. He's going to take it from the hospitals. Then they're going to turn around in five years and say, 'How come you can't run a hospital and make money." It's not a statement based on any side-choosing or political posturing. "We'll wake up in five years and the Democrats and the Republicans will start fighting again about who screwed it up. It is screwed up. We're all Americans. It doesn't seem like people care about that anymore."

Being mindful of the realities of healthcare costs, Anderson fears that the political aspects of solving the problem could bring a solution that could be excessive. "We're going to give medical care to probably a lot of people who don't even want it. You know a lot of young people say, 'I don't need medical care.' Is it forty million people? Is it fifty million? Is it twenty million? It's more like ten or twelve million. So, that's a concern of mine. The healthcare debate. The public healthcare debate."

Beyond safety, quality, and cost management, St. Luke's hasn't outlined specific action plans to address the proposed changes the Federal Government might impose. "You might say that's kind of irresponsible. Well, what we do is we keep our costs low. We try not to do things just to make money, even though hospitals all the time get accused of that. If we keep our costs low and we have good quality, then I think we're probably seventy percent of where we need to be." According to Thomas Reuters, the nation's leading source of healthcare information, these are not empty words to describe an abstract "feel-good" ambition to keep costs down. St. Luke's is ranked nationally among the most efficient in cost-per-adjusted discharge – meaning, patients there get more for less. He wishes it was an attitude that was shared by everyone in the cost chain. "One thing I can't figure out and something to ponder . . . we all have computers, cameras, whatever. It always seems the technology gets better and its prices go down. In healthcare it seems like the technology gets better and the prices go up. How does that work? Why are companies charging us more money? We're not jacking prices up because we're trying to make more money." He mentions a short list of technology companies whose pricing policies perplex him. "It's an interesting question. Nobody in the government has asked that question yet. Costs are through the roof. Healthcare is not cheap. We have a responsibility in healthcare to make sure we're not just providing the best and the latest and the greatest technology, but we've got to do it cost effectively."

If change is the only constant in the healthcare industry, what does Anderson see when he looks into the proverbial crystal ball for the Lehigh Valley? "The population is increasing. A lot more people are moving here from New Jersey and the Philadelphia region. One of the things The Valley and its citizens are blessed with is they have some really outstanding healthcare facilities available to them – not just St. Luke's. Our competitors do a great job of providing healthcare. They make us better – we make them better. It's very competitive. The competition in healthcare will continue – the quality will continue to get better and everybody wins on that. Whether through the government or just private initiatives like hospitals, I think you're going to see more and more focus on patient safety. Which again, everybody wins."

With population growth, also comes the need to address an increasing demand. St. Luke's Hospital & Health Network has purchased five-hundred acres of land between Route 78 and Route 33 in Bethlehem Township. Ground has already been broken for the construction of what will be among the most advanced healthcare facilities of its kind. "I call it the 'Nexus of the Universe.' It's the largest proposed healthcare campus I know of in the State . . . and probably the United States. So, twenty years from now, hopefully if I'm still around on the right side of the grass, there will be a pretty large series of facilities. Research facilities, a medical school, extended care facilities, acute care, and much more. St. Luke's will certainly be a leader on the eastern part of the United States. But, everything starts small and then grows. So, initially our phase one, we're going to build a hospital about the size of our hospital in Allentown, and then add to it as time passes. We're going to have a cancer care center that's about fifty-thousand square feet, also built with room to grow, and have a medical office building. That initial phase will be on about forty-five acres."

"Being on that much undeveloped land, there are so many opportunities. It's like having a pallet and you're an artist. You get to paint whatever you think will work. My view is if you can think about it and you can imagine it, you can do it. I've been telling our board to dream big . . . We have the money, we have the wherewithal to do it. It's going to be – we throw the word around - 'environmentally-friendly' or 'green.' We have a grant from the Commonwealth recognizing some of the environmentally-friendly issues that we proposed. We also have a pretty significant relationship with GE Healthcare. We are a GE Diagnostic International Show Sites, which means we have first access to the latest imaging technology available anywhere in the world. A lot of that stuff you won't be able to see. But it's there."

It doesn't take long to realize that Richard A. Anderson's words aren't measured for their sensational impact. He is comfortable speaking about things as they are – good and bad -with equal emphasis. Perhaps it's a quality that he cultivated as a scholar-athlete at the University of Illinois, where he competed as a swimmer in The Big Ten. His leadership of St. Luke's shares many of the qualities that aquatic success requires. A competitive swimmer doesn't hide from results and records rarely stand for long. Alone between the lane-markers of the swimming pool, the competitive swimmer develops an unwavering concentration that promotes introspection about every stroke, every muscle movement, and every possibility where self-improvement can be found. The thousandths-of-a-second by which champions are separated from the-rest-of-the-best develops emotional strength and an honest, no-excuses, self-awareness.

The CEO of St. Luke's still swims, several times each week, in what he describes as a way of releasing stress. However, it is easy to imagine that now his mind is reflecting on the mechanics of his hospital operation, contemplating the ways to move to the next decile of improvement, or neutralizing the vulnerabilities that threaten the hospital's standing. Or maybe he's thinking about the issues of the various civic causes to which he gives his precious time. He sits on the Board of Directors of the Lehigh Valley Industrial Park and Lehigh

University's College of Education Advisory Board. In 2008, he was the Honorary Chairman of the Salvation Army's Christmas Campaign. These are the activities of a transformational-minded leader compelled to "leave things better than he found them." The personal sacrifices involved in seeing such an ambition through influence the approach he takes in enjoying the golf game that gives him satisfaction during his private time.

"You need time if you're going to play eighteen holes of golf," so Anderson has adapted a game of golf that accommodates his competitive spirit and the demanding hours of his life. "I'll go home in these long daylight hours [the interview took place in August], and I can put a golf bag on my shoulder at about 6:30 and go off for about four or five holes by myself. My motto is 'hit 'em 'til you're happy.' If you don't get it up on the green on the first time, you drop another ball and hit another one. I have my own, 'better ball scramble.' " The most tenured CEO of a healthcare network in Pennsylvania describes the way he improves his golf game with words that could also be applied to the reason St. Luke's has become one of World's best healthcare organizations. "You'll be surprised. If you do anything long enough you'll get it right."

Take a look at the "before and after" image of St. Luke's and the appropriate words to describe the Anderson-led transformation don't readily come to mind. From one single hospital of understated value, it has blossomed into four full-service hospitals and one-hundred-fifty satellite facilities. Today it employs nearly as many people as it once cared for. It has been recognized as a world-class organization by the most discerning judging criteria in the trade. The future includes what will be among the most advanced medical campuses in America. Describing Anderson's string of achievements at St. Luke's as "awesome" is a disservice as long as that's the same word used by fifteen-year-old girls to describe a Jonas Brothers Concert. Yet, "awe" is what his record should inspire in even the most successful CEO's. It is an example of making the most of time, energy, and resources to deliver something few could have imagined on the outset.

Caroll Neubauer

Chairman and CEO of B. Braun Medical Inc

When Caroll Neubauer, the Chairman and CEO of B. Braun Medical Inc. talks about the heritage and culture of the Bethlehem-based healthcare technology company, it is underscored by his pride for what the company represents, and an optimism for what it can be. He has a genuine appreciation for the rare opportunity he has been given to guide an organization of measurable excellence. In addition to his leadership position for B. Braun in America, Neubauer also serves as one of the six

"Not managing the culture in a company is like not teaching values at home."

members on the Management Board of the German parent company, B. Braun Melsungen AG. It is a role he has had for nineteen of his twenty-two years with the company.

"It's a dream career. Something that could only happen in a private company - where the principal owner picks you and says, 'You're a young man, you have no experience - I'm going to give you everything you need. I trust you can do this.' After three years of professional experience he put me on the board of the B. Braun group of companies.

It's been a good ride - I hope for both of us," shares Neubauer. The ride, even from his earliest years, has been unusual – if not extraordinary. The son of a veterinarian, he was a grade-school boy in Wapello, Iowa and attended Boarding School in Germany. He followed his interest in law, passing the First State Bar Examination at Albert-Ludwigs-University, Freiburg, Germany and a few years later passed the Second State Bar Examination at State of Baden-Württemberg, Germany. Then he returned to the United States to earn a Masters of Law from Georgetown University in 1987.

With both US and German citizenships and a diverse educational background, he joined B. Braun Melsungen in 1988 to serve as the Legal Assistant to the CEO. He then became a foreign associate serving the Company through an exchange program with a St. Louis law firm. He returned to Melsungen a year later, headed the company's legal department, and with merely three years of professional experience, he was invited to join the Management Board. As one of only six members, he embraced the call to protect and serve the B. Braun family name that has been synonymous with excellence in serving people since 1839. Interesting as his personal story is, Neubauer isn't very interested in discussing it. Instead, he has passion in his timbre as he deflects the discussion toward the company's newest products, manufacturing advances, and the organizational structure that keeps the company focused on being preeminent. Neubauer, the company he has run since October 1996, and the people to whom he answers are a perfect match. He's a fit in a place where stability is the product of modest, smart, ethical, visionaries. In his time he's seen the company grow into a global healthcare technology leader. The lifeblood of B. Braun throughout the world is their ability to harness the necessary intellectual resources to ensure continuous innovation and advancement in the highly competitive healthcare arena.

When listening to the CEO talk about the company's trademarked "Sharing Expertise®" slogan, you realize that he's not just talking about fostering great intra-office communication - or even inter-office communication between the near two-hundred companies worldwide under the B. Braun masthead. "Sharing Expertise" includes gaining knowledge from -and sharing it with -patients, hospitals, and physicians, those in the supply chain, universities, and other technology companies. As part of the Management Board of a company that employs over 38,000 worldwide, and as the leader of one of its largest units, Neubauer sees how the "Sharing Expertise" slogan is working to guide the innovation that propels the B. Braun group of companies. It works because it has a solid structure as its foundation. "We have Centers of Excellence spread all over the world." Neubauer says these centers were established to take ownership of specific categories of products developed by the business.

"The Center of Excellence for urology is in France. The Center of Excellence for clinical nutrition is in Melsungen, Germany. The Center of Excellence for surgical instruments is in Tuttlingen, Germany. And the Center of Excellence for needle-free infusion therapy and implantable spine products are right here in The Valley." Neubauer explains that these Centers of Excellence gather information from all corners of the world. "Innovation is what drives medical technology companies. Physicians want progress - there's a lot of progress to be made. Physicians want the newest and best products, particularly in the areas where we work. If you're not innovative you'll be out of business in due course. How do you do it? 'Sharing Expertise' is exactly what it's all about. 'Sharing Expertise' with our colleagues in China, with our colleagues in the UK, with our colleagues in Brazil . . ."

The organization links the employees in these places to benefit from all the knowledge and expertise they can contribute. "They all work with physicians. They all work with companies that have intelligent solutions that they are trying to bring to us that we have to develop. It's a culture of having to innovate to have a sustainable business model." It's a collaborative structure that pays off in sustainable dividends - the company outperforms nearly every standard for judging a business. Even during the worst global financial and economic crisis since World War II, the family-owned German company's Chairman of the Management Board said the B. Braun group of companies was "largely unaffected." Prof. Dr. h.c. Ludwig Georg Braun, attributes this to the company's "conservative, long-term approach to business management." They are cautious about the unstable economic times, yet in recent years while others pulled back resources and reduced staff, they have increased their research expenditure to leverage competitive strengths against the great opportunities they see. In the

Lehigh Valley this cautious optimism is visible in new facilities and investments. "We built an R&D center in Tech Park up behind Fogelsville and are bringing new innovative products to market. Have you seen our Marcon facilities? It's a huge plant that just extended its capacity by fifty percent. We bought the Surefit property, thirty-four acres next door as well. B. Braun is here to grow. We have some new products also coming in from other B. Braun organizations which we've developed and are now going through U.S. clinical trials." He says distribution centers are not the place where he wants to invest in the company's future, so they are rented as needed.

"I'd rather spend our money and put our eggs in a basket of building a manufacturing facility or buying twenty new injection molding machines, manufacturing with 'clean rooms' and special technology. Our new state-of-the-art injection molding facility over at Marcon - I expect that to be on the front page of Industry Week Magazine in due course. It's injection molding in a leading edge 'clean room' environment, which is absolutely, completely new, it's special, and it's really highly advanced. You won't find it anywhere else. It's modern technology in manufacturing." As Neubauer speaks, you hear a competitive imperative to be vertically integrated that cycles right back to the "Sharing Expertise®" trademark. There is a real understanding of the ultimate use. "These devices are used on people." That imposes a level of responsibility to ensure products are safe, validated, and have guaranteed, consistent quality. "Developing and having ideas is one thing. Getting that product out in a cost effective way is what we also do extremely well. We even do a lot of in-house development of our machines because that's also know-how that some competitor can't immediately say 'I'm going to go over there and buy that same machine and make that same product." In addition to structuring a network that keeps more than 38,000 employees worldwide 'Sharing Expertise,' B. Braun invests in creating the environment that grows loyalty to the company.

"To have a competitive advantage it is critical to cultivate a workforce with the will to persevere and stay committed to the dynamically challenging standards-of-excellence in healthcare. Our employees are our most important asset. That is it. Our employees make the Company" Neubauer says. In the Lehigh Valley B. Braun exhibits its appreciation of employees in a range of ways. "We have an executive suite at the Iron Pig stadium, but no executive uses it. We actually raffle it off to all the employees." The company's Iron Pigs executive suite was a way for the company to help the community's fledgling baseball team and to support a quality entertainment asset of the Lehigh Valley. Because B. Braun is a healthcare company they are prohibited from entertaining clients. Using the suite for an employee perk parlays their investment in a way that strengthens the company spirit. But the baseball suite raffle is only one example to demonstrate a culture of employee appreciation. "We just worked with one of the fitness centers here. We bought a membership for every employee. Any B. Braun employee can go 24/7 to one of the group's fitness centers and can utilize all of the facilities. They love it. It keeps them healthy. They've got something to do in their spare time. That's B. Braun. That's an environment where you'll find the innovation that you're looking for, where you find people who will go the extra mile for the company, because the company goes the extra mile for them." From his words, you realize that the B. Braun culture is as important to their competitive positioning as their products and manufacturing innovations. Neubauer says, "Not managing the culture in a company is like not teaching values at home." This is an entreaty learned from his first years at B. Braun of America.

Caroll Neubauer arrived with his family to preside over the company's American unit in October, 1996. B. Braun Medical Inc. was a company he knew -a $200 million niche player in a huge American healthcare industry. The company was comparatively small, but doing very, very well. "Then, within two months, we started to negotiate the acquisition of a much larger company -McGaw, Inc. in Irvine California. We started our discussions in the end of November and finally closed on that company in May. A $200 million company bought a $350 million company. The 1,550 employees grew to 4,400 employees. It changed the whole game. It changed my whole life. It changed this whole organization - the goals and everything that went along with it. Wow, was I surprised." With McGaw under its wing, B. Braun Medical Inc. was not just a bigger operation, it was a management nightmare.

"You're talking about two different worlds. We had the mars people and we had the moon people. This was a total culture clash." McGaw had always belonged to larger organizations. The company was regularly turned-over or sold, and over the years its employees saw a string of new owners come and go. "McGaw went through twelve different hands in twenty years. Loyalty and all that was nothing that really counted." McGaw was nothing like the company he came to America to run. "B. Braun Medical Inc. had always been a small operation, operating on its own, playing its niche game in the United States. There was a strong loyalty to the organization. There were hardly any changes in management since we acquired it in 1979. You're talking about two different worlds - opposites - that's exactly what we were. To be honest, from the moment of the acquisition until 2001 and 2002, we had a hard time - economically, organizationally, structurally.

"We switched eighty percent of the management. We had to replace, we had to merge, we had to integrate. We had to bring things together. McGaw was quite a run-down company which needed a lot of investments. They had nothing in the pipeline. We had to restructure, re-strategize, and develop brand new tactics to make it work." Looking back, Neubauer is pleased with the end result. "I enjoyed building the team I have today. We used the existing management, brought in new management. Today I believe we're one of the leading management teams in healthcare, but of course I am biased! And that was fun building, but on the peripheral, there was a lot of stress . . . a lot of nights that I couldn't sleep." While the acquisition and transition of the company since the McGaw deal ranks at the top of his achievements, Neubauer, is also quite satisfied by another initiative he set out to complete.

Neubauer says that before arriving, and when they were a small niche-oriented company, USA had been "a bit of an island." Today, with approximately $1.25 billion in revenue and 5,500 employees, they've become an important, respected, and connected part of a huge group. They're the conduit to America for B. Braun products originating from every corner of the globe. They make products for the rest of the world. "We're much more integrated in the huge network of B. Braun group of companies. We've set a foundation for B. Braun Medical Inc. to continue to be one of the leading healthcare companies in the United States. And that foundation I would say is very solid."

Also on a solid foundation is B. Braun's commitment to the local community. It's something Neubauer says might have been at risk after the McGaw acquisition. "My colleagues on the board were quite convinced that the larger company had to be the headquarters, as you can imagine. It had a beautiful and impressive headquarters building in Irvine, in Orange County, California." The CEO argued that, "What B. Braun represented was more here than it was there, and I wouldn't have gotten everybody down there."

He explained that the quality of life for the employees in Orange County, even with a cost of living adjustment, would not match the quality they could enjoy in The Valley. Not moving was also better for business in terms of serving customers. "We're in a better corridor here - our pharmaceutical, medical device, bio-pharm corridor is better here." And of course, there's the "Sharing Expertise" objective hindered by the nine-hour time difference. "When the Germans go home, the Californians haven't even come to the office yet. Here we only have a six hour time difference. That gives three or four hours that overlap to communicate." There is video communication equipment in Neubauer's office that is tied to a worldwide network of offices via the company's data lines. "I can talk to twenty different offices alone in our [German] headquarters. It's perfect. It's like you're sitting in the office of those people. With that, Sharing Expertise is live. It's much better live than through email communication."

While he can recite a range of practical business arguments to keep the company's home in the Lehigh Valley, it would betray no secret to say there is a strong personal reason for staying put. "I love this community. Anybody who knows me knows how much I cherish this community. My wife, my son, and I all love the Lehigh Valley." He's lived in the Lehigh Valley longer than all but one of the many places he has lived. This is where his family calls home.

"One thing the Lehigh Valley can be extremely proud of is that after the decline of the steel business, the fathers of this community have done an excellent job of fielding a diversified industry and diversified business structure. We have the infrastructure. We have the universities." He likes the location for its convenience to all of the major metropolitan areas where he does business. For example, New York and Philadelphia are convenient by car. Flying from the convenience of the Allentown airport, Chicago is ninety minutes away. He is deeply interested in reviving travel to and from The Valley by rail, committing some of his energy to help the group that is trying to make it happen. "If you could go to Philly or to New York just with the train - how many additional people could we bring to The Valley?" The train is just one in a range of Lehigh Valley issues or concerns where the B. Braun "Sharing Expertise" mentality extends beyond the business to help the quality of life in the region.

"One thing that we've found out in our 171 year history is that corporate citizenship is something very important. It's not only good for the environment where we live; it's also good for the organization. It's good for our employees. If it's the Chamber. If it's in the Railway Committee that's trying to bring the train. If it's in the Lehigh Valley Partnership - where I sit with many of the other CEO's of The Valley, some of the politicians, and others - to find ways to work with the government, to do the right things, so our valley can prosper. We work with the colleges. We have interns from the engineering schools in our manufacturing facilities. We actually have scholarships to the nursing schools here." The company donates to the arts, gets involved in community development projects, and provides support for projects that bring improvements to the local quality of life.

"Worldwide, we have the B. Braun for Children Program. Every organization in the B. Braun group is obligated to have a program of some kind to help children - be it educational, be it housing, be it food. There's so much to it, we could talk about only that during all the time we have together. Those kinds of things are part of our corporate understanding to help our communities flourish."

This community involvement isn't directly rewarded in the way an ice cream shop might benefit from supporting the local Little League team. "Ninety-two to ninety-four percent of all hospitals in the US buy products from B. Braun. So, we're here in The Valley but The Valley is not our major customer." He reads a paragraph from the B. Braun Group Strategy and B. Braun Group Charter. "B. Braun is aware of its responsibility as a 'corporate citizen,' and we will fulfill this obligation to the best of our ability in all of our corporate locations worldwide. We have a professional responsibility to our customers and a social responsibility to our employees and the regions in which we conduct business." To manage this professional and community responsibility includes mitigating any uncontrollable threats that might hinder the company's health. Today Neubauer sees real complications that temper his optimism emerging from Washington, DC.

"It just shows you how optimistic I am to be maintaining optimism with what's going on in Washington, DC." He recognizes there is a problem in the US healthcare system and can intelligently discuss the meaningful ideas to address them. But in the end, the actions taking place in DC are going to potentially cost his company tens-of-millions of dollars that have no hope of being recovered. "It's absolutely concerning. It's not only concerning for my organization, but for my customers, the hospitals and the physicians. It's concerning for all. We're supposed to be hit with an excise tax on top of our sales for no reason whatsoever -except to finance healthcare. We're not going to pick up any additional business. Our patients -the acute care patients - are being treated today anyway. You go to an emergency room you have to be treated and the hospitals pay our bills. Nevertheless it will cost us a lot of money -all money that I can't put into innovation, and new product, and a new facility, and on-and-on. It's hard to maintain optimism looking at what's going on -but we've been through 171 years and seen a lot of changes. We will survive these changes as well."

Neubauer steers the B. Braun business in America. He sits on the board of the parent company. He also gives his time to other local companies, community organizations, and causes. Are there enough hours in a day for him to have time of his own? "I'm a person that does not rest well. That's a problem; I'm constantly on-the-move. I'm a horrible golfer. But, I honestly love the game. So Saucon Valley Country Club is where you'll find me on my weekends when I'm here and maybe even on some summer evenings when I get out of here early enough. I also have a place at Pinehurst in North Carolina where I go to when I'm not in The Valley. So between those two places - that's just about what I do." Not one to rest much, he does occasionally parlay his business travel into brief escapes. "I'm in Europe a lot. I have to travel fifteen to seventeen times a year, so I also use that to stay in Munich for the weekend, or take my family and jump down to Rome or some European metropolitan areas. The German Black Forest is a place I love to go." As he talks, you realize he steals time for himself that he might not actually miss if he didn't. Neubauer is a man who loves his work, his company, and the industry in which he works.

He's quite young, as CEO's with his years of experience go, and he has spent a career disinclined to see his company statically. So naturally, when asked how he wants to be remembered when he finally does step away, his answer is a bit reluctant. "I've got a lot of years to go so I don't spend too much time thinking about a legacy that I'd want people to look at once I'm not doing what I'm doing. But if I look at it now, and what I want people to think tomorrow about what I did yesterday, I would be very proud to see that I laid the foundation for B. Braun of America to be a leader in healthcare, a sustainable leader in healthcare, particularly in infusion therapy, which is my kind of passion - that we are known for bringing innovative and the highest quality products, as the leader of the healthcare company that built that foundation on a sustainable basis."

Considering his path, he just could be the embodiment of all the best qualities associated with the places where he was nurtured – "down-to-earth" Midwestern practicality, the German passion for excellence, and the analytical mind of a Georgetown lawyer. His path prepared him perfectly for the family-owned company, where the next quarterly sales results are less important than preserving a family legacy. Through his leadership, the Lehigh Valley has enjoyed the fruits of B. Braun of America's success through new jobs, new revenues, and a community-minded spirit that makes the company a cherished regional asset. He grew B. Braun USA from $200 million to $1.25 billion in under fourteen years in an acutely competitive industry. Positioned for a limitless future, the corporate charter ensures every B. Braun advancement will make life in the Lehigh Valley better.

David Jaindl

Jaindl Family Farms

"I never had an interest in doing anything but working in the farm operation. As a youngster I worked very closely with my grandfather. It's the only thing I remember." David Jaindl's grandfather was his real-life role model, the person he hoped to emulate. When other youngsters wanted to be

"Absolutely there is conflict . . . You need that. We don't always agree, but we always end up agreeing."

cowboys, firemen, doctors, or astronauts - David wanted to be a turkey farmer. Things might have turned out differently if they spent their time together fishing. But working in the business is how they bonded and the farm is where they found their joy.

"I spent a lot of time with my grandfather - from eight years old, nine years old, ten-years-old. Learning turkeys. Learning the mechanical side. Learning construction - because he was a top-notch carpenter in his day. In summers I'd wake up in the morning and drive with him to where they'd be loading turkeys at five o'clock in the morning. He'd do nothing but talk and teach. It was always pleasant experiences working with my grandfather." As he got older he spent more time with his father. "Working with my dad on the business and the land development side I certainly learned a lot. My dad and I spent six hours a day together, six days a week. I think we all - me and my siblings - got a lot of exposure to my father. He taught us a lot. Hopefully he taught us enough that we could carry things on in a positive direction."

The Jaindl story starts with five turkeys purchased at a county fair in 1935 by John Jaindl, David's grandfather. At the time he also purchased five ducks for his daughter. "My dad took the turkeys and started raising them," David says. His dad, Fred Jaindl, was a high school student at the time. From the original five turkeys, he and his father grew and expanded the operation. By the time Fred was discharged from military service, the farm was growing twelve-hundred turkeys annually. But at that time, they also raised cattle, operated a small orchard, and the family owned a small bar and restaurant just outside of Allentown. Turkey farming was just one of the things they did.

"I think my dad was always the catalyst for the expansion. My dad was the aggressive one. He knew land and he knew banking, and so he leveraged one to buy the other." The direction the expansion took moved the company step-by-step toward a totally integrated operation. "They had a hatchery in the early '50's that they built. In the late '50's they built a processing plant." They focused on quality. Fred Jaindl's selective breeding skills produced a turkey that gained renown worldwide. The special broad-breasted breed produces as much as 54% more white meat than the typical bird. The National Turkey Federation awarded the first Blue Ribbon to Jaindl Farms in 1954. For over forty years, Jaindl's "Grand Champion Brand" has been selected by the National Turkey Federation for Thanksgiving at the White House. In 1965, Fred purchased the farm outright and John stayed on as the General Manager. They were producing 200,000 birds and farming 500 acres of land at the time.

In 1980, David took over the General Management of the farm, and with his father, they continued to grow, adding more land to farm, expanding the hatcheries, increasing their processing capacity, developing more land, and acquiring Schantz Orchards. After the passing of his father, David purchased the operation. Since 2005 he has continued to manage it in the family farm tradition with his siblings. Today they produce over 750,000 turkeys each year while farming over 10,000 acres. David talks about leading the company bearing the family name. "Are there pressures? Sure. But the pressures are minimized because of the amount of experience I was able to get through my grandfather and through my father over all those years. What you have to remember is that for twenty-four or twenty-five years I had been effectively managing the operation. My dad had all the headaches; we all had our own responsibilities - myself and my siblings. There were really no surprises. My dad's passing, of course, was a big surprise to all of us. But as far as running the business and taking on that added responsibility - there wasn't a lot of added responsibility."

David Jaindl emphasizes one key point. "It's not a one-man show." The way he describes it, he oversees a workforce that to a large degree was raised in farming with him. "We have family members watching out for different aspects of the operations. The general manager of the farm operation has forty-five years of experience. He grew up in the business, also." It's a management scenario in which the connections between the staff members are woven in respect, time and trust. "The way things get done is to have good people working with you. You have good management, good family members, you have experienced staff. It's not done by one person."

"Besides Cathy (Jaindl-Leuthe, his sister) on the inside with the land development, and Richard Gildner on the farm side - who has been working here and managing here for forty-five years - I have a nephew, John Jaindl, Jr., who is an assistant manager on the agricultural team who does a great job and who I depend on more and more." He has two sisters and a brother who work seasonally and part time. "I have four sons, two that are working full-time and learning the operation and two that are a big help during the summer and holidays, as they are still in college. My daughter is in high school and she helps out seasonally. On occasion we do bring management expertise in, such as our health and nutrition manager. But normally our management learns from the ground up."

Does learning operations from the bottom up give them all the same perspective? Can people growing up together in a business have diverse points-of-view? "Absolutely there is conflict. But conflict is healthy. The senior management team gets together and we bounce ideas off each other. Because we're doing so many different things, every day there's something different with the agricultural side, with the turkey side, with the orchard, with land development. There's always something going on. We all get together and we look for input from everybody."

As an example, David discusses a recent decision regarding a new bag design. "If I did exactly what I wanted and what I thought was right it wouldn't look like it does today. It looks great today. Mine was okay, but with the input we got from everybody else, and all the feedback from the experienced people around that table, it was really productive. You need that. We don't always agree, but we always end up agreeing." To tell the boss that you might have a better idea can be career suicide in some cultures. How does David maintain a culture that permits free and frank dialog so the outcomes are the collective best the company has to offer? "That's easy. Of the people involved in our senior management, there's nobody trying to kiss up to me. They've already earned their place. They all have a strict and strong position with the organization. They have a lot of different ideas, good ideas. And in a lot of cases, better ideas. That has never been an issue. My dad felt the same way."

Over the years a lot has changed to improve systems and increase productivity. The labor to produce 800,000 turkeys now isn't as intensive as it was for his father to produce 200,000 birds in 1966. Today the operation is largely automated. The turkey processing facilities are capable of shipping as many as twenty tractor trailer loads of product daily. The hospital-clean hatchery is capable of incubating 450 thousand eggs at any time. They farm over 10,000 acres of company-owned land to grow soy and corn for feed grains. The Jaindl-owned feed mill can produce 1,800 tons of feed for the turkeys each week. The bio-diesel processed on-site fuels the farm equipment and heats the buildings. The capacity to do all of this is based on modern equipment and machinery. Yet, there is one aspect that machines cannot replace. The breeding stock that produces the unique broad-breasted quality is handpicked from the Jaindl flock by David in the same medal-winning tradition established by his father. "Just as my father before me, I still select each breeder that parents next year's offspring."

Turkey farming is inherently a Thanksgiving-focused enterprise. Having the majority of the business focused on one day of the year creates some special issues for managing the company. Jaindl's year-round operation depends upon eighty fulltime employees. The company adds part-time employees in the summer. To process and ship for Thanksgiving, seventy seasonal employees are temporarily brought on board. "Clearly, if we could stretch that capacity throughout the year, it would be great. You can put this into perspective - from January right on through September we're distributing one to two tractor trailer loads a month. In the month of November we're distributing up to twenty-a-day, seven days a week." He puts it another way. "Seriously, if you look at that - January through September, one to two trailer loads per month, forty-thousand pounds per trailer load. In the month of November, we're doing three-hundred-fifty [trailer loads]."

The business in the non-Thanksgiving months depends on frozen turkeys, which are not exactly a staple food item like hamburger or chickens. Frozen Turkeys are slower turning, lower volume product that makes it vulnerable when the economy sags and distributors are concerned with cash flow. "What we experienced in the first and second quarter of '09, after the downturn of the economy, was that very few distributors were buying frozen turkeys as they normally do. They didn't want to put the money up. They didn't want to buy the turkeys, inventory them, and then sell them. They were 'hand to mouth' with the cash concerns because they just didn't know what was going to happen. So, we experienced that, we had to adjust, and we did adjust. But, this year - 2010, it was a lot different than the first two quarters of last year. In a good way."

The state of frozen turkey sales from January through September might be a sign that the economy is improving. But other areas of the Jaindl enterprise show there is still a way to go. His discussion of the company's land development business is tempered with realism. "It's been an awfully cold land business for the last two years. We feel its going to rebound. So, if you ask how I feel about the land business now - a lot better than I did a year ago. Is it where it should be? No. Do we aspire to see it where it was three or four years ago? That's a long shot."

Part of why land development may not concern him greatly is because of how the community has been positioned for growth. He could be a spokesman for the quality of live and the vitality of the Lehigh Valley. David Jaindl believes the region has more to offer than ever. "I really think the Valley has a great image right now. Certainly it could be enhanced. For job creation - we have all the social values here in the Valley. It's proximity to New York and Philadelphia is great. There are a lot of areas you can live in the Valley. It's very different. Within ten-minutes you can go from very rural to very active areas. Geographically you're very close to the Philly area and the New York area and that makes it attractive for business to come here. I know with some of the struggles that New Jersey is having right now, a lot of companies are looking strongly at Pennsylvania, particularly the Lehigh Valley because of its proximity to the New York markets and the availability of good labor here in the Valley. It's always been a great work ethic with the men and women in the Valley. I think businesses know that. The ability to attract other users here for more jobs is important. But, I think it's already built into the Valley."

As he talks about the real estate and land development market, he keeps things in perspective. "When it comes to looking back at what you're doing - the agricultural side is what's most important. To see that the agriculture side continues is important because it's the foundation of our whole operation. The land development is important. I can't discount the importance of our land development company. But effectively, turkeys and agriculture are most important."

He does like to talk turkey and agriculture. The products, the processes, the people, and the history the preceded his taking the reins of the company are very comfortable topics. Ask him what he's done to put his fingerprint on the business he says, "I really can't say that there's one thing." He has to be reminded that the introduction of bio-fuel processing, the CAK System, and Organic Products all happened under his ownership. "Beating his own drum," he admits, isn't something that comes natural to him. But his leadership has led to some exciting new advancements.

"The bio-fuel is important. When everybody was talking about 'green,' we were already doing it. We weren't doing it in a big way, but we had the installation of the presses, and the process, and the conversion to a bio-diesel in advance of all that green talk going on." The fuel Jaindl produces is enough to operate farm machinery and heat their buildings. There were Government grants available to purchase the equipment, but Jaindl did not take any State or Federal grant monies or any taxpayer dollars. Not doing so is simply fits the character of the company. "We had a little bit of a leg up, as opposed to others. If we didn't have the infrastructure in place - the storage bins and the capacity, the grain elevators, and the transferring equipment - we couldn't have made it work. If I needed taxpayer dollars to put the presses in, I just felt that it would have been trouble from the start. It's just the way we feel."

Since David Jaindl took ownership of the company, they also introduced an innovative turkey pre-process to replace the traditional electronic stunning method. It's a more humane, but costly, nitrogen gas process they call the CAK System (controlled atmosphere killing). "We think that's a big advantage. The equipment was designed by our own mechanics and engineers in-house. The expertise for exactly how it was to be designed and implemented was collected from many people in the industry throughout the world. We had one of our top men handling that." The company worked with Air Products to implement the system safely and properly, developing what David says is a very good partnership. "Working with Air Products keeps it in the Lehigh Valley family. Our system is exclusive to our operation. Nitrogen is more expensive, but it's a better way to handle the turkeys."

The Humane Society endorsed the process with a letter that was sent to retailers encouraging them to buy turkeys from Jaindl. The record will show that the humane handling the birds is important to the farming operation. Every year they take part in an animal welfare audit that rates the company on how well animals are treated. "We're proud to say we have rated high in our scores every year we've participated. We rate in the high 90's. The evaluators tell us that the typical score is in the low to mid-80's."

As an accommodation for some of the company's larger customers, in 2009 Jaindl Farms became certified organic. "We grew 20 thousand organics for last year and have orders this year for about 35 thousand." The demand for organic products is gradually moving from the fringe to the mainstream. Addressing this segment takes much more than a boardroom decision, new packaging, and a slick ad campaign. There's a lot of preparation and investment to comply with the strict government oversight and regulation or organic farming.

"To do organics, first the farm has to be certified organic, which we are. Then, if you want to grow organic turkeys you have to have organic feed. So we go to a feed operator who is strictly domesticated organic feed. We buy our feed from them." To offer organic products requires that Jaindl Farms deviates from their vertically integrated business model to buy third-party feed. That will eventually change. "At this point we don't grow organic grains on the farm. Once you designate a farm you want to go organic, it takes three years to wean-out the chemicals that are in the ground. Then you can potentially have it certified for organic grain. We already have some areas in both Northampton and Lehigh Counties that we want to consider converting to 'certified organic.'"

After talking with David Jaindl for a while, you start to realize that he favors taking a positive perspective regardless of the topic. "We're very positive people around here. You have to be. In agriculture, you see no rain coming and the crops are drying up, you have to be positive." Even discussing the intense government regulation and oversight of his industry evokes no ill remark. Is Jaindl Farms hindered by too much government interference? Does regulation put them at a disadvantage against the giant national food producers? "We're certainly not at any advantage. And I don't think we're at a disadvantage. When it comes to what processors are required to do, it's pretty much the same across the board. According to food safety, we're all under scrutiny - which is a good thing. It allows American food manufacturers to be producing the safest food in the world. Is there a lot of oversight? There's a lot of oversight. Is there more oversight than there was twenty years ago? Ten-fold. Is it a bad thing? No."

Businesses large and small often complain about too much government intervention and regulation. David, the constant optimist, sees the silver-lining. "All plants are very safe. The regulations the Federal Government have implemented in this country are second-to-none." Perhaps he isn't bothered by regulators because the government's standards don't rival what Jaindl Farms imposes on themselves. In the Jaindl hatchery all eggs are washed, sanitized and air-dried in special washing equipment within one hour after they arrive. Unlike other commercially grown turkeys, each newly hatched Jaindl flock is placed on totally fresh bedding in a barn that has been cleaned and sanitized to ensure a productive, disease-free flock. "The way we process our turkeys, the water system we use with fresh water as opposed to recycled water, minimizes and concern for bacteria on the turkey. When you do that it adds shelf life and is better for the consumer."

"Better for the consumer," David will say. It makes sense that serving consumers better would be the foundation of a stable business. At the end of every Jaindl innovation is ultimately a benefit. Organic birds and all-natural turkeys with more white meat and less fat and are better for you. Humane treatment of animals may cost more, but it's the right thing to do. A vertically integrated organization that produces feed for its animals and fuel for the equipment means lower input costs, a better consumer value, and a reduced environmental impact. "We have expanded into different lines. Organic as you know. 'Antibiotic Free' which is taking off. We've also expanded into some further-processing items. Boneless breast product, turkey barbeque, boneless smoked turkey, smoked legs, smoked wings - retail items like that. We're expanding that and are looking to expand that more in the future. Some of the product - the organic fuel, the soybean oil that we are producing - we have been selling that 'off-farm.' We've been using a lot to capacity, but there is a big market for that type of product so we have also been selling it. We can expand it, but the production of bio-fuel really falls in-line with the proteins [processed for the turkey diet]. The younger turkeys use a low-oil protein meal. We squeeze the oil out. The older turkeys use what we call a full-oil meal - that is the oil is left in the protein. So the availability of the oil we derive is based on the turkeys that we grow."

The growth and success of the Jaindl family businesses over the years has produced one of Lehigh Valley's most active and visible corporate citizens. The Jaindl name is seen throughout the Lehigh Valley. Hospital Buildings, highways, and other impressions reflect a family that is engaged to help the community . "We have the Fred J. Jaindl Foundation. Myself, two of my siblings, and my mother meet on a regular basis and the focus has always been the aging and the children." He is fundamentally involved with the Miracle League, which is a baseball program for the mentally and physically challenged children and young adults in the Lehigh Valley. The games take place at a field that was built three years ago. Taking the initial ballpark concept and creating something tangible happened very quickly because the right people were involved. "Lee Butz, Kostas Kalogeropoulos, and I brought [the idea] here to the office three-and-a-half years ago. The following December, right before Christmas, Lee and I went out to look at some sites. I took him to a site that I thought made some sense. I took him through the process. I hired an engineer. Got it approved in very quick fashion - sixty days. We started construction in April and on July 22nd or so, we had our first game - it was all built. Cathy is on the board with me at the Miracle League. A contribution to the Miracle League is so justified - a couple dollars go a long way because so many folks who give in-kind. A little bit of capital goes a long way." To see physically challenged children experience a game that they could only dream of playing without the program - and to see the student-volunteers who make those dreams come true - is very satisfying. "If you go up there and just watch a game for an hour - it's an experience. And it's not only the three-hundred kids that are serviced. It's also the three-hundred volunteers, the high school kids that experience that. They have a different outlook on life."

David and his family are active in the community, giving their time and treasure to do what they can, when they can. It has been reported that his typical workweek falls between seventy and eighty hours. He admits that leaves very little time for anything else. What does he do for recreation? "Not much," he smiles. "It's long work but I enjoy it. We don't go on a lot of vacations. But my down time I spend with family. I have five children and a great wife. So, when I'm not working I'm with my family." He seems content. It's enviable when you think about it. He goes to work every day doing exactly what gave him joy as a nine-year-old boy. He's a turkey farmer just like his grandfather. What could be better than that?

Dr. Alice P. Gast
Lehigh University

Dr. Alice P. Gast, the President of Lehigh University, is perfectly suited for a community like the Lehigh Valley. She is a catalyst for transformation in a region where transformation has been the operative word since the demise of the steel industry. She fits in an environment where extraordinary leaders from the thriving local companies, the world class hospitals and the groundbreaking nonprofit sector have created one of the most vital economies in the Northeast.

"It's so important to figure out what the community needs and wants and not what you think they want."

It is not hard to see why she appealed to the university's Board. She is wonderful in the art of conversation and expresses ideas in words valuable enough to ponder. You get the sense that she is where she wants to be.

Dr. Gast has great regard for the extraordinary qualities that were at the foundation of the institution that she became part of four years ago. Yet, she has brought new eyes to see that more is possible. More importantly, through a broad-reaching study of community attitudes, she has discovered that her hopes and wants for Lehigh are shared. "There were a lot of devices and approaches to get people to write about the history of the future," Dr. Gast says. The result of this exploration was a consensus that ten years from now Lehigh University could be ranked among the greatest educational institutions in America. She came here as a world renown academic leader. Sitting comfortably between a career heavy in achievement and the lofty ambitions she has blueprinted for the university, she is confident that Lehigh will rise to match this new vision.

Lehigh University's was founded on the principle that combining a scientific and classical education would produce an educated workforce that could rebuild America after the Civil War. Dr. Gast's aspiration to graduate men and women who are prepared address the critical local, national and global issues of tomorrow is perfectly aligned with the vision of the founders. To fulfill the responsibility of producing tomorrow's problem solvers, she encouraged the Board to allow the institution to move "beyond the historically acceptable level of risk" and make "bold moves" so that Lehigh University could become "a leader in learning, a leader in innovation, and a leader in creativity." Dr. Gast recommended leveraging the institution's strengths in a mission that is summarized in four words – "advancing our intellectual footprint." She introduced ideas that were supported by months of comprehensive information gathering and the undeniable energy of students, the faculty and staff, the alumni and the community.

Let us ratchet back just for a moment. She used the expression, "The history of the future," when asking the community to imagine the possibilities of the next ten years. It is an expression worth savoring. It recognizes that the best way to plan going forward is to imagine what you want to be and then plan your actions so that when you look back everything you do is righteous. In this case, it ensures that all actions compliment the school's traditions and add to the legacy of all who came before them. It's an expression that gets individuals to think about their own legacies and how they will augment the finest values of the school. The strategic planning process, Dr. Gast says, "Was an opportunity to ask the entire community to step back from the tyranny of the immediate, to step back from their day-to-day work and all the things they're worried about – and even what they are worried about months from now – and say, 'What do we really want Lehigh to be about ten years from now?' By thinking together as a community about the future, you really develop a strong sense of who you are and what you want to be."

The report she presented to the Board in July 2008 was entitled *Transforming Lehigh: Advancing Our Intellectual Footprint.* It explored four themes: enhancing the student life and learning experience; responding to vital challenges through research and graduate programs; investing in the staff and faculty necessary to be at the forefront of distinguished universities; and partnering in the Renaissance of the local community. The plan published in 2009 is intent on making Lehigh University increasingly relevant in a shrinking world. "Universities are not known for changing rapidly. But the world is changing faster, and we need to change faster now."

In August 2006, Dr. Gast came to Lehigh knowing a thing or two about what it takes for a university to become an academic leader and a premier research institution. She was the vice president for research and associate provost at Massachusetts Institute of Technology from 2001 until summer of 2006. She was the Robert T. Haslam chair in chemical engineering. For sixteen years before that she was a professor of chemical engineering at Stanford University and at the Stanford Synchrotron Radiation Laboratory. Her awards for advancement in scientific research put her in one of the most exclusive peer groups on earth. The short list of achievement includes the National Academy of Sciences Award for Initiative in Research, The Colburn Award of the American Institute of Chemical Engineers, the Camille and Henry Dreyfus Teacher Scholar Award, and a Guggenheim Fellowship. She co-authored *Physical Chemistry of Surfaces,* a classic textbook on colloid and surface phenomena. She was involved in the Bio-X Project at Stanford that resulted in the Clark Center for Bio-Medical Science and Engineering. "It was a new approach to bringing in interdisciplinary teams, breaking down walls in the building, and having people really interact by mingling research groups and things like that."

She says making the decision to move from being a professor to being an administrator was not easy. "I'm a professor who always viewed my graduate students as my product. We did some great research. We understood and developed some new knowledge and learned new things." However, it was preparing students to advance into the world to solve problems and to have enriched careers that the professor enjoyed most. "I knew I'd have fewer of them as I moved forward in this job." It was Bob Brown, the President of Boston University and the former provost at MIT, who helped her see that coming to Lehigh would allow her to provide broader opportunities to even more students. In the way Dr. Gast is able to discuss specific students at the university and the things they have discovered about campus life she continues to seem connected to the student community and the various achievements and activities in which they are involved. Perhaps this desire to know her students and the ways they are growing positively is an aspect that makes her the natural leader within the "Lehigh family" culture.

She talks about the family feeling that is embedded in the Lehigh culture. "I'm familiar with enthusiastic alumni in all the schools I've been associated, but here there's a special Lehigh family feeling. You see it in the way they continue to help us out. In this recent job market the alumni network has been incredibly important for our students finding jobs – and finding career paths – not just jobs. Connections. Advice along the way. Mentorship. They just willingly give their time and energy to that. They also help us recruit students. We can call upon our alumni to have send-offs all over the country – they are such enthusiastic ambassadors for the school. I guess I hadn't really seen that at that level before." There is a grin on her face as she speaks of the alumni. The energy they give to the school and commitment to the young graduates actually surprised her.

Of course, running the university is running a business. The financial model of a university is complicated and in so many ways dependent upon the success of others. When businesses struggle, as government budgets tighten, and as the securities markets dip. Things like funded research through grants and contracted support, the endowments and alumni gifts could be negatively impacted. Because Lehigh University is more dependent on tuition as a revenue source than its aspirant peers, it is fair to wonder if there have been any significant setbacks caused by the current economic conditions.

"We're still on plan. We actually finished our capital campaign last December. We do see some people needing to wait and putting their plans off a little. But our donors are very supportive and generous." Additionally, while revenue growth is critically important to see the complete plan through to fruition, many of the specific action plans are based on applying in-hand resources and intellectual capital more strategically. "We're really moving into implementing the strategic plan through a lot of dialog and activity on campus. We can make sure we are hiring faculty to move us in the right areas, engaging our students from the very first year and making sure they get connected to all the different things that they can do to have the highest-level experience."

Engaging students in their first year is among the most important tactics to produce the strategic-thinking, inductive-reasoning, problem solvers of tomorrow. Of course, students need to be in class, studying their lessons, finishing their projects and scoring well on exams. They need to be given the tools and conditions that ensure their success in whatever they endeavor. However, cultivating a workforce to deal with tomorrow's issues demands more than teaching the newest theories and the latest answers. "We get great students. My concern is that students come into a university these days so driven and so hyper-focused that you really need to convince them to unwind a little bit. Branch out, take different courses, join a club, be in a music program, be in our athletics program and really have the richness of the inside and outside the classroom experience."

Dr. Gast believes that the socialization aspect of living in college and learning to work with people from different backgrounds, with different interests and who are studying different disciplines is critically important for society. "Our role as a residential university is more important than ever. It is an important life experience. We could all stay electronically connected and have distance relationships via Facebook and texting and not be able to have a very effective meeting where people understand each other face-to-face."

Answering the need for an educated generation that will be equipped to contribute solutions to the future problems of the world is the goal that drives the complete educational experience at Lehigh. It's why students are put in situations where what they learned in theory is practically applied to solve problems in the community or industry. At Lehigh students work as a part of multidisciplinary teams so they get used to the way others work and think. Students get the eye-opening and invaluable experience of attacking real issues through projects that are initiated in cooperation with, or on behalf of, the local municipalities, leading corporate neighbors, local entrepreneurs and the school itself. In one example, a team of about twenty students from disciplines are diverse as business, engineering, architecture and humanities designed Lehigh's athletic facilities - including the double-sided stands with the lacrosse and soccer field and the new golf practice facility. In another example, "We had a student working with a professor here, and a person from St. Luke's, on surveying the region for asthma presentations at the emergency room." Dr. Gast said this study uncovered not just a healthcare concerns for the hospital to address, but a range of other environmental, sociological and educational issues.

In many ways, this practical approach to education that Lehigh calls the "Integrated Learning Experience" contributes to the renaissance of the local community. "A group of civil engineering students went off and helped Bethlehem design an expansion of their sewage treatment plant. Students are going to work on the greenway - the South Bethlehem bicycle way. They're going to work on the gathering spaces to meet the community's needs, where to put community gardens, where you can put art." Applying new knowledge, working with others from different disciplines and learning to be a contributing part of a self-directed work group also leads to learning life-lessons. "I quoted a student in my commencement speech who said she learned in town how you really need to listen to their needs and what they want. It's so important to figure out what the community needs and wants and not what you think they want."

Being involved with the revitalization of Bethlehem's south side is practical for the school beyond being a laboratory for student projects. To attract the best students and the most esteemed professors and researchers, it is important to be able to offer an attractive quality of life. The strategic plan describes the vibrant street life, the mix of housing, the eclectic shops and the lively arts scene that provides the climate for a flourishing community. "We have a strong sense that the intellectual community should transcend the boundaries of the campus. Part of that is having your own people living in the area. Part of that is engaging the people who already live here. We're doing both. We're really looking at how we engage the community, how we help the community think about its future. There's a lovely merchant district, but it struggles. It is struggling in this economy. It was struggling before this economy. There are opportunities for us to help small businesses think about what thrives in a region where we have a relatively small university. There are certain types of businesses that do thrive in a neighborhood like this."

Lehigh University is very involved with the area's schools. Dr. Gast is enthusiastic about their participation and support of the "community schools" concept. The concept includes after school programs run by professional educators that support the specific curriculum being taught in school. Community schools are places that deal with family health, employment issues and other situations addressed by social service agencies. "The idea of the community schools concept is that families are often reluctant to go get services from other government agencies. But, they'll all come to their kid's school. You're able to help the whole family. To help the kids you have to help the whole family.

We're very excited about that."

Dr. Gast says that while the community schools concept is labor-intensive, a lot of people want to help. "Look at all the philanthropic money going into K-through-12. Everyone's recognition is that the future is in education and these kids." She says that universities have a huge role in supporting community success in this area. "We have the Center for Developing Urban Educational Leaders which has the Saturday school at Central in Allentown." The concept is to bring the teachers in on Saturday morning to share new ways of teaching literacy. Later, you bring in the kids so the teachers practice what they just learned. Finally, the parents join in and learn what they need to know so they can take the books home and help. You create a partnership with the teachers and the parents and the children.

"Our Center for Developing Urban Educational Leaders is also working with principals." The idea is to provide support to life-long educators that suddenly become administrators. With the Lehigh University's program they get help with issues like running a school with a transient population or dealing with unions. In Philadelphia, principals from the urban academies are thriving through a Center for Developing Urban Educational Leaders program that supports them with mentors from the business community. "There's hopeful progress. There are certainly grand challenges out there. I do think it will be the students educated at places like Lehigh that can help us tackle them."

The Lehigh University ten-year strategic plan exemplifies the best-practices in organizational leadership. It addresses grand challenges and national needs in three strategic areas of focus: globalization; energy, environment and infrastructure; and health. In invests in a strategic expansion of the faculty and staff. It sets the framework for a best-in-class student experience and a promotion of student success through core competencies. Finally, it plans to partner in the renaissance of the community. It draws from the strengths of the university and its faculty to have the most significant impact on the world. It focuses on preparing graduates to compete in a rapidly changing global community. Every goal is tied to metrics that measure success. They will track how the institution improves scholarly outputs in referenced journals, books published, and its faculty awards. They will measure the number of research grants submitted and the rate for which they are awarded. The expenditures per faculty by source will be tracked. The marketability of the school's reputation will be gauged by the quality of graduate school applicants and the outputs they yield in terms of advanced degrees. In fact, there are over one-hundred specific measurements that will be tracked that ensure the mission of "advancing the intellectual footprint" is clearly understood and communicated throughout the organization.

There is a systematic quality to both the plan and the report card that naturally leads to progress that begets more progress. As the institution is able to raise more money, it will be able to attract the most elite professor/scholar/researchers, so it will be able to mine new knowledge, so it will be able to increase its publication outputs, so it will attract the most sought after graduate students, so it will be able to increase its revenue stream, and so on. There's a systematic rhythm to the annual cycle of things that leads to a logical snowballing effect. In a way, the most critical element to accelerate the cycle was to bring a scholar/researcher/author like Dr. Gast to lead the university. She won't say it out loud, but as she describes the school's endowed chair strategy you realize how she is the catalyst that sets so much more in motion.

As a renowned scientist, researcher and educator, Dr. Gast's own reputation is significant in recruiting the best talent available. Think about that as she talks about the value of finding donors who will endow a chair. "If you can bring in a key intellectual leader you can catalyze a lot more so you can get an amplification of the chair. The chair is the leader, the person, the intellectual leader. But they also attract other faculty. Junior faculty positions will be filled because they want to work with this person." Are there specific endowed chairs that Dr. Gast would like to attract to the university? "It's so important for us to be able to frame our broader goals in the real role of the professor. The research they do, the new knowledge they create, the scholarly work, and the students they educate who will go on and take their new knowledge on to their careers and to the rest of the world. It is incumbent on us to frame those in ways that are not too narrow.

"The value-added of a chair allows you to attract a better level of talent or a person who will be particularly a catalyst for more at the University. As I told one search committee, you really want to attract the kind of person that everybody wants to run into in the hall and have a conversation. The kind of person, who when talking to them, helps you generate your own ideas by making you think."

Not long ago, Forbes published some very interesting statistics regarding college presidents. Nationally, only twenty-three percent are women. However, of the universities that Forbes ranks among the top six in the country, three are run by women. "Women bring particular skills. A university is a very collaborative, collegial environment, so it's very different that running a corporation." Dr. Gast says leading a university requires the ability to listen to different perspectives and understand why a person may have the perspective they do. The academic leaders she admires are good meeting a contentious issue, understanding why there is disagreement and then helping people understand that what's good for the whole is good for everybody. "It's an organization and structure that doesn't lend itself to top-down leadership. It takes a different type of leader."

Another notable statistic regarding college presidents is the difference between the percentage of married men and married women that lead institutions. Eighty-nine percent of men and only sixty-three percent of women are married. Dr. Gast is married and has two children. "I love spending time with my family. I have two teenaged kids – fourteen and sixteen. Spending time with them is a huge priority. My daughter is in track, so free time means going to track meets. My son just took up Alpine skiing. They run cross country." Her husband, Bradley Askins has an interesting and accomplished story of his own. After pursuing an AB in History at the University of Southern California, he developed an interest in complex modeling systems that led him into graduate studies in computer science. He spent most of his career managing research and project engineering teams at Hewlett-Packard in the Silicon Valley. Today he is a computer consultant. "He's started doing some pro bono teaching in the CS Department and he loves that," Dr. Gast says. "He loves interacting with the students. He taught a new data mining course - think about all the interesting projects that spin out of that for community and otherwise when you have data and can understand it better and use it. He's involved. He co-leads the Vision 2014 with the Mayor, is on the Bach Choir Board, and things like that."

When Dr. Gast speaks about her husband you could conclude that he is the model that encompasses all the qualities that she wants to see in her graduates: able to lead teams that solve complex problems; joy for learning and exchanging knowledge; giving time to the community. "He also does things with the kids. I'm blessed with his tremendous support." The job of running a university is demanding and time consuming but Dr. Gast says, "I don't miss really important stuff. One thing I miss doing is we used to cook together a lot more." She says her children have somehow forgotten that she actually does know how to find her way around the kitchen.

When spending time with herself she likes to run. For a time was sidelined due to knee problems, but after reading a book called "Born to Run" about the Indians in Northern Mexico who run long distances, she's taken up "barefoot" running complete with the weird five-finger shoes that her daughter doesn't like her to be seen wearing. "When you pound on your heels you hurt your knees. But, when you run barefoot you tend to land on the front of your foot," she explains. She loves hiking, but since her family isn't as avid as she is, that seems to be reserved for vacations and special occasions. "On my birthday I get to go on a hike," she says with a slight chuckle. Finally, her latest interest is fly fishing.

This is an example of the teacher following her own expectations of her students and wadding out of her comfort zone. "I'm not very good at it, but it is fun to learn." It is interesting is to listen to her explain what she finds most appealing about fly fishing. She contrasts the experience against the realities of learning golf where being a novice among better more experienced players can be a little stressful. The seasoned fishermen are happy to share what they know. They are patient people with encouraging advice and an eagerness to help. What she enjoys about her new sport is aligned with the theme that threads throughout everything she says is important about effective education. It brings out the best in people. "It's nice," she says.

Dr. Christopher Bennick

Habitat for Humanity

There are times when Dr. Christopher Bennick sounds like an entrepreneur. At other times he sounds like a social worker. The CEO for Habitat for Humanity of the Lehigh Valley is, in fact, a strategic thinking land developer focused on helping families that deserve a break. Between entrepreneur and social worker Dr. Bennick owns a seamless melding of competencies, experiences and beliefs that have been perfect for leading the local Habitat affiliate.

"An organization, if it is constantly growing and improving its processes, in two years it will be a different organization

Once a grass-roots nonprofit on the verge of bankruptcy, the local Habitat is now a study for organizations of any kind to emulate. He talks about collaboration, continuous change, creative empowerment, and strategic planning processes in the real context of his organization's success. The core of his conversation focuses on the families that ultimately own Habitat-built homes and on the children that may otherwise not have a chance for success. The story about the man himself almost never sneaks into the dialog, but when it does it helps to understand his motivation. "I grew up poor. We didn't always have food. I had to wear my dad's socks for mittens. But, we always had a home." It isn't something on which he dwells, preferring instead to discuss the mission of Habitat. "Studies show that children that grow up in a stable home environment are more likely to stay in school. They have a place to do home work. They graduate. They're less likely to be involved in drugs, teen pregnancy and continued poverty. It is all tied to the home."

The leader of any nonprofit can talk about the values brought to the community, the volunteers, and its donors through their organization's work. Dr. Bennick would rather show you. "Other nonprofits have to say, 'This is what we're doing.' I don't have to explain it. You can come out and see it. It's not about building a low income housing project. It's about strengthening a community or renewing a neighborhood. Last year we built twelve homes in the worst economic downturn that the world has ever experienced. Our goal is to do the same thing this year." There are individual homes that have been built by Habitat throughout the Valley. Yet, the most profound example of the organization's potential is exemplified by its current work on Bethlehem's south side. "Over the last several years I have been working on this development [in Bethlehem]. We raised funding and bought this parcel of land. It is approximately eighteen acres. Combined with several minor subdivisions nearby it provides lots for forty houses. At the same time we preserved twelve acres of the mountainous wildlife.

"The south side community started around the 1890's when the steel started. As development worked its way up the mountain, they just built one street after another. In 1929, the majority of the building stopped." The Great Depression ended the construction. Habitat's development is actually completing parts of the original plan of 1929. It is happening at a time when other investments to revitalize Bethlehem's south side have brought a new casino, the entertainment complex and an industrial park. New jobs are arriving in the south side community while record unemployment cripples much of the country. "We provide an opportunity for people to live, work and recreate in their own city. That's called Smart Growth." For their development on Bethlehem's south side, Dr. Bennick and the local Habitat affiliate were recognized by the Commonwealth of Pennsylvania for visionary leadership in building community collaborations that support Smart Growth. "It is that concept that we are trying to duplicate in every city across the Valley." In fact, as work is being completed with the current development in Bethlehem, there are plans for a fifty-home development in Allentown and a block of homes in Easton.

"I run a charity. But I also run a business." It is worth noting that in the interview transcript for this story, Dr. Bennick used a total of 7,062 words. He used the word "charity" only once. It's probably because his organization doesn't give handouts. If you are going to live in a Habitat-built home it won't be given to you. Families earn them through a combination of sweat-equity, instruction through required classes, mentoring, engaging in community service, and ultimately paying back a mortgage. A family must be motivated to meet some very demanding qualifications before being considered for a home.

"We select families on three criteria: need, the ability to pay and the willingness to partner. They cannot already own a home. They have to be in an income bracket that is below sixty-percent median income. We develop a partnership with them." Partnership, indeed. To receive a home the process usually takes a couple of years. There is a family selection committee that qualifies applicants for Board approval. If the Board approves them they are required to put in fifty hours before they are assigned a home.

"To me, we are changing generations after generations of these children - we are changing their lives. We are breaking that cycle of dependency, poverty and the system in general." Dr. Bennick emphasizes one of the most important facts about the relationship between Habitat, the families they serve, and the homes they build. "This is a long term commitment to changing someone's life. We hold an interest-free mortgage. Our volunteers and donors dedicate their time and resources. Because of that, we have a vested interest in making every family in the program successful. We consider the homeowners our partners which is probably why of the eighty-five or eighty-six homes we've delivered we have had zero foreclosures."

When he first started with Habitat, Christopher Bennick did not appear to be the natural choice for the job. "I had a Masters in English Literature and had worked for the Bethlehem Police Department," he says. While at the police department he wrote a lot of grants and served on nonprofit boards which gave him a basic idea of how nonprofits operate. After retiring from the department, he offered the Habitat executive board a proposal. "I told them that I wanted to start a doctoral program in organizational leadership that would apply to running a non-profit." He convinced them that he could participate in a program in Sarasota, Florida that would entail intense weeklong on-campus courses in such areas as team management, leadership, communication, motivation and conflict resolution. Each course would be followed by a research project.

"I told them that I would bring each back to the organization, look at our strategic plan, look at where we want to go, look at the different committee structures, and I would implement doctoral theories to improve efficiency and grow the organization. For his dissertation, Dr. Bennick researched leadership traits and 'high performance' to determine why some Habitat for Humanity affiliates perform at a higher productivity level than others. "I studied the ten highest performing Habitats on the east coast. I flew to each of their locations, interviewed them, surveyed them, looked at how they ran things, and brought the good elements back to my executive team and said, 'Okay, how we implement this here?" Dr. Bennick also did post-doctorate executive education at Harvard Business School, studying nonprofit management, community collaborations, and other areas that could add excellence to Habitat's performance of their mission.

A model for managing the Lehigh Valley's Habitat with a very low operating cost was developed by Dr. Bennick and the Executive

Board. It calls for a very small, professional staff with the rest of the work done by volunteers serving on the various committees. There are about one-hundred-fifty core volunteers that work for the affiliate. "I like to call them 'teams,' but it's a committee structure. Once we forge our strategic plan, everything rolls into it. You have your five-year goals rolled into a one-year operational plan." If the goal is to build twelve homes, each team has its own individual goals that tie back to how that will be accomplished.

"Six months prior to building a house there is a lot of planning to be done. One team needs to recruit and process a specific number of family applications knowing only a few will qualify for the program. The funding has to be in place. The materials must be on schedule. The volunteer labor must be organized. If the bulldozer guy doesn't show up on schedule, you could have twenty volunteers who took off work standing around a build site unable to work. Each of these major functions is managed by one of the dozen or so teams. "We build in safeguards. We try to have backups for everything. In general, it's just contingency planning. Everything has three plans. If one fails you go right to the next plan."

The local Habitat operates at a 90% efficiency rate—meaning only ten-percent if its financial resources go to the administration of the program. Charity Navigator, a national organization that ranks non-profits, places the local Habitat among the top ten-percent of all US non-profits. Dr. Bennick says to be nationally ranked is a bragging point only earned by leveraging the volunteer and professional staff's talents, skills and resources to achieve a common mission.

"Seven years ago we had two dilapidated crack houses and maybe a building lot or two. We now have close to fifty building parcels. When I first came on-board we refined our work processes, upgraded all our technology, and revamped our accounting system. We grew over four-hundred percent in five years while applying sound strategies and leadership theories. We are always looking ahead a couple of years to where we are going and strategizing how we are going to be able to develop it."

Partnerships are formed with potential homeowners, with the volunteers that build the homes, with the teams that execute the strategic plan, and with the financial donors. "It's easy for me to say 'write me a check.' I don't want that," Dr. Bennick states. The strongest partnerships are the ones in which those who want to support the cause find something in the program that also helps them. "We have corporations that come out and use the build as a team building exercise. There's a whole learning process about working together as a team, doing something you have never done before, and feeling successful about it in the end.

"Or let's say you have a summer camp or a church group of kids. You could build a lesson into it—that some kids don't have homes. You could take pictures or build a slide show or a movie about Habitat. They could get together items to bring to a home dedication. Sometimes volunteers build flower boxes and everybody brings a plant for the family—so even the youth are involved at that level. For adults it doesn't matter what age they are. We have a whole group of retirees that volunteer on-site a couple times a week, every week of the year. It builds camaraderie amongst them. In the summertime when we have an accelerated blitz build, some of the elderly women like to make the food for the construction volunteers. There are also lawyers and CPA's donating their services. We actively engage everybody. We're always looking for ways to involve more people. This combined effort enables us to be successful. We have some great people from some of the major corporations actively involved in our mission. People are motivated—not for money—but to come out here and change somebody's life or to make a legacy investment. I am just trying to be a good steward of everybody's desire to do that. I watch every single nickel so everything is as efficient as possible."

To some, "watching nickels" might be translated to mean producing a product that is just good enough to meets Habitat's mission to build "simple and affordable" homes. Yet, the spirit behind the volunteers that build Habitat homes is too powerful to let mediocre construction happen. "There was a big hurricane down in Florida years ago. The storm came though there and wiped out a bunch of homes. All of the Habitat homes remained standing. When Katrina happened, a lot of the Habitat homes in New Orleans didn't have much damage." Dr. Bennick says the reason these homes endured such catastrophic storms rolls back to the mindset of the volunteers who give their time. "The volunteers are so dedicated to building a good quality house that if you try to skimp corners that's like a sin to them. Everybody wants to hammer nails, so if it needs one nail, it probably has three."

He says Habitat is no different than any other builder when it comes to inspections and approvals. Except, being a non-profit has allowed another partnership to develop. "The city not only gives funding for land, but they also help us understand the approval process and get us through that. Maybe some of the inspectors come out a lot quicker because they know it's a blitz build and it's accelerated, but that's just another building partner that we have." Another participant to improving quality and increasing efficiency.

"I manage from a 'constant change management' theory. An organization, if it is constantly growing and improving its processes, in two years it will be a different organization. That means you have to bring new people, new talent on board. You have to identify where your weaknesses are and bring resources in to help. That means, as the organization changes you will have, by natural attrition and selection, new people in and other people out. We try to keep a balance between social worker types of volunteers that want to work directly with families, business people that understand business, finance, and how things work, and those people that don't care about those things but just want to build a house. If we get too many people on one side or the other we need to balance it out. It is about having good people in the organization—getting the right people on the bus." Once the "right people" are in place, the mission is carried out by self-managed work teams. It is a management style in which the people closest to the tasks require only a minimal level of direction and enjoy seeing their ideas contribute to something valuable. "This is how it works...they can go, 'Okay Chris, this is how I think I can do this task or accomplish this goal.' And I can say, 'Maybe tweak it this way and then run with it.' Now, that person isn't just doing a job. They're going, 'I get it. I'm part of the big picture. My idea is helping. It's working. And I'm running with it.' I call it 'performance-based leadership with creative empowerment.' A lot of non-profits do not do this. A lot of businesses do not do this either."

It is a management philosophy based on inclusion. The strategic goals and objectives provide the framework for everyone's success. "Everyone can feel important and everyone can know they are part of the bigger plan. Everyone is paddling in the same direction." Teams of volunteers understand their responsibilities and how they tie to the bigger plan. "If a team isn't really aligned with the bigger plan you have to have a discussion, 'Listen, if you head in that direction you're not going to be able to accomplish this part of our plan. These are our goals.' Sometimes people are involved with non-profit because they want something different than the Board wants. But our mission is to build simple, affordable homes. You cannot have mission drift. You cannot have them doing things that are not focused on the plan, focused on what we have decided at an organizational level as to where we are headed. I can lead the organization but I cannot do that without the help of a lot of other smart people working in unison to effectuate the mission."

It's no surprise that Bennick's doctorate is of the Ed. D. variety. The educational component of his degree fits his coaching and mentoring leadership style. "A lot of times I use the words 'Continuous Process Improvement' or CPI, because a lot of the local corporations use that kind of theory. But isn't that just basic Peter Drucker? 'How do we do what we are already doing better?' I often have that discussion with my different teams. We are always trying to improve. It is not that we would be doing a bad job if we planned to build twelve houses this year and we only built ten. Or, if we only raised $2 million. Or, if we only helped ten families or thirty kids. That is still success. But we must be strategic and continuously ask, 'How do we do it better next year?' That is how you create an atmosphere of continuous growth and continuous change. If people cannot get used to continuous change you cannot grow." Dr. Bennick once taught a seminar on change at the national conference. He talked about initially managing a $500,000 budget and building three homes in a year—and over the next five years growing to raise $2,000,000 annually so twelve homes could be built. He talked about how that necessitated adding 5,000 more volunteer opportunities into the process. "You think it is not change to grow?" he asked. "If you didn't change to grow you could never adapt or accommodate the needs of the bigger organization. You have to be willing to change, to learn. It is critical to growth. You have to continuously improve or you will stagnate."

There are elements in the national program that actually force growing affiliates to constantly recruit new volunteers and sponsors. "The good thing about the Habitat model is that it recommends not taking more than 'x-percent" of funding from any one source. If we were a quasi-government nonprofit agency that depended on a lot of money from the State, if the State ran out of money the programs would stop. Or if we were dependent on one wealthy donor, and that donor decided this year they want to give to another organization, our program stops. We do target marketing. We look at all of the different groups. We look at how they could be involved." Dr. Bennick is constantly monitoring each segment of the community that supports his affiliate. "Whether they are individuals, corporations, churches, foundations, grant writing, or events, I'm just looking at 'How do we take a balanced approach to this.' How do we actively engage each segment of the community? We must ask ourselves, 'What is it that the city wants to see happening in their community? What do prominent individuals like to see in their particular city or the Valley? What is the motivation for a church or a corporation to be involved in our mission?' I craft a targeted strategy. Then I pass that concept onto the different teams in our organization and they run with it." Dr. Bennick says that understanding what is appealing to each unique segment of the community and how that fits the Habitat mission works to create solid, sustained partnerships. "When we look at our strategic plan or our business development and marketing plan, it is clear that there is a certain portion of the Lehigh Valley that understands that a larger group serving the entire Valley can be more efficient, have less overhead, be able to tackle problems on a larger scale and be able to leverage a greater amount of resources. Many politicians, business leaders and others approach planning this way. But there are also people that say, 'I care about center city Allentown,' or 'I care about

Bethlehem,' or 'I really care about Easton and I'm focused on that—I really want what I do to go to this particular city or this particular area of the city.' There's nothing the matter with that. That's great. We are currently forming a leadership group that wants to do block building in Allentown—a coalition of people who are really Allentown-centric. We are looking to form a similar group in Easton. Those are new people who will come into the organization, they will bring other friends and they will have a lasting impact on their local community. The more you can have people from one of those groups on some other team that's looking at the bigger picture—that's even better. You cannot be successful without a variety of groups."

The Habitat mission is to construct a new future for needy families by providing the benefits of home ownership. "Our families are taking a proactive approach to helping their children have a better life. If we can get them a home through any other program, we serve as a referral source and help them into that program. But, typically our families are below sub prime and cannot get a home any other way. Because of Habitat's work, a family with a combined total income of $12 an hour can afford a new home. In this economy, we are successfully building homes for the most needy of children and families, we are changing their lives in a meaningful way, and we have had zero foreclosures. That is a great bragging point for our local Habitat. Not every affiliate can say that." The Lehigh Valley Habitat affiliate has also proven to be a great way for the community to come together to do good. The growth of the program, the success of the volunteers and their impact on the lives of more and more families is worth celebrating. "When we finish a house we dedicate it to the homeowner. We invite all the volunteers and the sponsors that helped build the home to a small ceremony. The kids are playing in the yard. The mom cries." When Bennick talks about it there's a crackle of emotion in his voice. "It's touching to witness this, to be part of it," he says. Dr. Christopher Bennick smiles. Sure, there are times he talks like a land developing entrepreneur with a restless vision for growth and expansion. Yet at other times, like when he talks about the presentation of a home to its new residents, he's just seems satisfied.

For more information on the Home Building Program or to donate, visit www.HabitatLehighValley.org or call 610-776-7737.

Greg Butz

Alvin H. Butz Inc.

Try to imagine the times. It was 1920. Woodrow Wilson was in office as the last President elected before voting rights were guaranteed to women. Prohibition was declared in effect. The Red Sox had just traded a pitcher named Babe Ruth to the Yankees and Shoeless Joe Jackson was never to play again. Jack Dempsey was the Heavyweight Champion of the World. The national population boomed to fifty million. Industrialism was the symbol of American prosperity, driven by the steel industry that

"We try to operate so that if somebody has a problem they can come to me - just like if somebody in a family has a problem."

placed the Lehigh Valley among the most prosperous areas of the Country. That was the environment when Alvin H. Butz hung his shingle and started the company his grandson manages today. It was a long time ago.

It is hard to think of another company that has made such a tangible impact on the Lehigh Valley landscape as Alvin H. Butz, Inc. There is a building somewhere in the area that stands to mark every period of life

101

in The Valley since their beginning. They have built the region's colleges and universities, hospitals and healthcare facilities, industrial plants, churches, prisons, stadiums, theaters and so very much more. If you have a meeting in an office, they probably built it. They probably built your favorite library or the municipal building where the business of your community is managed. And while the official history of Alvin H. Butz, Inc. records the company's beginnings as 1920, according to President and CEO, Greg L. Butz, there's a bit more to the story behind the Lehigh Valley's oldest construction management company. "I'm actually a fifth generation builder. My great, great grandfather was a builder. He built a lot of the covered bridges in the Lehigh Valley."

Butz understands how unusual it is for him to be at the head of a company his grandfather started, let alone continuing a family tradition that began two generations before that. Passing and preserving a family business through generational changes is very unlikely. "It's hard. Not too many of them make it to the second generation, and something like 10% make it to the third. There are statistics, and they aren't very good for how long a company is going to last." Greg Butz has two sons and a daughter. His daughter is in the fashion industry, one son is in college, one in high school. "The boys have some interest. We'll see what happens." The President and CEO presiding over the family legacy is a man following his heart. "It started probably when I was four or five years old. I'd follow my dad around. My dad would go out on construction sites on the weekends and I'd tag along with him. He talked about it a lot at the dining room table - about his customers and situations.

"So it's almost like a forty-five year training program I was in. It's something I grew up with everyday - hearing him and the family talk about work - it was kind of a twenty-four hour a day thing." In 2007, when his father stepped into an advisory role and named him CEO, he was well-trained and perfectly prepared to carry the company into the future. "I was a laborer in high school. I was an assistant superintendent in college. When I got out of college I was a superintendent, an assistant project manager, and a senior project manager - so I've done almost every job in the company. By the time I got to be the CEO I can't say that there was anything to surprise me. I'd been pretty much training for it since I was a little kid."

Asked if anything surprised him after taking on the CEO's responsibilities and he mentions something that a rare few would understand. "There's some pressure because you're the fifth generation - pressure to make it succeed and get on to the next generation - you feel that in the back of your mind. But there certainly wasn't anything surprising in terms of job description kinds of things that would come up because I've been doing it so long and [my father] had trained me so well. Since I was a little kid, he talked about how important it was to satisfy the customer, and how important is was to get every job completed on time, the quality level to keep and maintain a reputation -I knew those things when I was ten years old."

He did have a moment as he was leaving college when he did flirt with the idea of not jumping into the company business. Like his father before him, Greg Butz was an athlete. "I had some brief, brief thoughts of playing baseball. I played at Lehigh and had some thoughts of giving that a shot. But I just decided the opportunity was probably better with the family business." His love for baseball didn't end upon graduation. He continued playing in a semi-pro league in the Lehigh Valley where he was a shortstop for the championship Allentown Wings and the Allentown entry in the Blue Mountain League. In October, 1995, he was inducted into the Blue Mountain League Hall of Fame. The honor was recognition that he was a good ballplayer who may have had a chance in pro ball. Yet, he doesn't show a hint of regret as his practicality (something he also must have inherited from the Pennsylvania Dutch values of his elders) explains, "The life of the baseball player in the minor leagues . . . It doesn't usually work out too well. Like I said, since I was a little kid I always pictured I'd follow my dad's footsteps, so I never really pictured doing anything else."

Over the years, the company has always evolved and responded to the opportunities and challenges of the times. They pioneered the construction management concept in the area in 1973, and now employ a staff that includes engineers, architects, CPA's, MBA's and some of the most experienced and capable project managers and field superintendents in the industry. There is a full-time safety director on staff, as well as highly-skilled carpenters and cement finishers.

Since 1981, the regionally-focused company has been consistently named among Engineering News Record's top 100 construction managers in the country. In 1995, when his father Lee assumed the role of CEO, Greg Butz took the reins of the family business as

President. Since then, he has put a few of his ideas in motion. "We expanded our territory into Philadelphia, Harrisburg, and State College about seven years ago. We saw a need to grow to be able to compete with the big national companies from an expertise standpoint" A larger organization generating revenue from a wider regional base brought with it the resources to add talent in some of the more specialized areas necessary in order to win the challenging high-profile projects normally awarded the national competition. "We just completed the Las Vegas Sands project. That required personnel from our Harrisburg and our Philadelphia offices to be able to do something of that size." Spreading their reach beyond the Lehigh Valley has proven to be a smart tactic for further deepening the company's foundation and stability - the company's regional diversification has been especially important during the tough economy. Few industries have been hit as hard as the construction business.

"To diversify from a location standpoint is actually turning out to be a pretty good thing now. Sometimes when we're not as busy in the Lehigh Valley, we could be busy in Harrisburg, State College, or Philadelphia. There are always ups and downs in the construction business. It's just a natural thing. Sometimes you've got a lot of work and sometimes it slows down a little bit." With the company established in four different regions, it has been able to produce a more constant income flow, smoothing the peaks and valleys of their volume. "That's probably the biggest thing, so far as 'putting my stamp' on something." He acknowledges that business could be better. "The depression eighty years ago was probably the last time we went through anything like the way it is now from a challenging standpoint - from not enough work out there." Is there recovery in sight? "I think we're seeing a little bit of it. Like a few months ago, the banks and money were tight. Even if you wanted to build something you couldn't do it because of the financial situation. I think that's loosening up a little bit - but we've still got a ways to go. There are quite a few projects that were put on hold that haven't started up again. We've still got a bunch of work -with Lehigh University, Muhlenberg College, the Allentown School District, and ArtsQuest - so we're getting through it better than most. But it's challenging. The next couple of years are going to be slow."

In spite of the current economic challenges, Butz has a lot of confidence in the Lehigh Valley. "There's unlimited potential for the Lehigh Valley over the next five years. Our location is tremendous with the highway system and how close it is to Philadelphia and New York and how quickly you can get to those places. You can see some of that with the companies that are coming into the area. Olympus choosing the Lehigh Valley. Las Vegas Sands seeing this is a place they wanted to be. It's all about location. New York and Philly are busy places that are encouraging change and growth in our direction. You see it in the residential area - it's amazing how many people live in the Lehigh Valley and work in Philadelphia and New Jersey. Our area has tremendous hospitals and colleges. The baseball stadium coming here and now the hockey arena. The quality of life in the Lehigh Valley is great."

He stands firm in his belief that there is no better place to run a company. "The work ethic is tremendous in the Lehigh Valley. That's an advantage of our company. Our employees. We've got the best construction employees in the world working for our company. It's challenging right now. Obviously with the recession and the economy there's not a whole lot of work going on. A lot of industries are challenged at the moment. But when it comes back it's going to come back in a big way. It's going to keep growing -there's no way it's not going to keep growing."

Being born, raised, educated, and nurtured in the community, he sees to it that one of the company's business principles is to buy locally, hire locally, and support the local industry as much as possible. "As much as we can we try to keep the local products and local companies involved. A national contractor will come in and not care as much about using local people as we do. I think that is one of the advantages in the Lehigh Valley with a company like ours, we keep using local subcontractors and suppliers. Ninety percent of the contractors for the Sands project were local contractors. There were a couple of specialty things that you couldn't get in the Lehigh Valley. But we had really good people." Always on his mind is also to use the products of the area's largest employers. "Lutron and Victaulic are products used on many of our projects."

Greg Butz does have one concern that troubles him in regard to the continuing revitalization of the Lehigh Valley. He feels strongly that more needs to be done to stimulate the Allentown urban core. But, true to his character, he isn't simply talking about it. He has taken action with a first step he hopes others will follow. "We had a really nice office out in the suburbs. It was a great location and it worked well for us. But we just decided we wanted to do something more significant to help the community. We saw the economic revitalization of downtown Allentown as a key thing for everybody in the Lehigh Valley. So I made the decision with my brother Eric to do what we thought was really important to help Allentown."

Alvin H. Butz, Inc. moved their offices to the eight-hundred block of Hamilton Street in Allentown. They built a modern six-story office building to house their operation -with plenty of additional room to attract other businesses to the downtown area. "We did it to try to help the community - and to do something other than to build a six-story building. We occupy two of the floors here and we are trying to attract a lot more people downtown, to hopefully get a lot of other companies to jump on the bandwagon and do the same thing." At the moment the building is now the home of several community organizations focused on the town's revitalization. "The Chamber of Commerce, the Convention and Visitors Bureau - they see being in downtown Allentown as importantly as we see it. It's great for us that they are in the building. It's a little disappointing there aren't a lot more businesses. We did a pretty good job of attracting those kinds of groups, but I was hoping to bring businesses from the suburbs into downtown. It's been disappointing and challenging - we're still working on it and I have hopes. "

As he talks about his commitment to Allentown's downtown area, he recognizes that there's a stigma that needs to be overcome. "There's a bad perception of being in downtown Allentown - and most of it is perception and not reality. People think it is dangerous walking out there. If you go out at two o'clock in the morning it might be a little dangerous. But it certainly is not dangerous at lunchtime." He talks about the vitality along Hamilton Street and the surrounding area. He describes a special quality that you can enjoy in the city street at lunchtime that those in the suburbs never get to see. "It's fun working downtown. It's fun walking to lunch every day. In the suburbs you have to get in your car and drive somewhere. A lot of times you just brought something in or it was brought for you. Here it's great to be able to walk out, to see people walking around. It's a great atmosphere."

Bringing businesses and the people who work in them, back to the city is one of the first steps Butz believes is critical for creating the environment that will attract young professionals to The Valley. "The urban core is a big part. In Philadelphia and New York, the kids like to live downtown. Here we don't have the downtown revitalized the way it needs to be. We need more housing downtown. But the housing doesn't come until you have some of the amenities. So we need to start out with the businesses, the restaurants, and the culture - and then the housing will have to follow all of that. Kids want to live where things are happening. Twenty-two year old kids don't want to be in the suburbs. They should be downtown." To spark a movement toward a revitalized downtown the Butz family has put their money where their mouths are. "That's why we are trying to do what we're doing down here and why others need to jump in and help with the downtown." His vision for a vital downtown Allentown is a forward thinking vision that will attract the young professionals to the area who will ultimately be important in providing the skilled workforce to support the local corporations and regional economy of the future. Yet, today Butz has had no problems in getting just the right kind of people his company needs in order to compete with anyone.

"It's not hard to recruit talent. We're doing most of the big jobs in the Lehigh Valley, so most of the best construction people will want to work for us if they want to work on big, exciting projects. We may have challenges competing [for talent] against a big national company. But, we also operate the way a family business does. There are a lot of advantages, as opposed to a big company where you have lots of rules and regulations. We're able to be a little more flexible. As I've said, we have the best construction employees in the world. To use a baseball analogy, we have an All-Star team. We have the best employee in every position that we could have." What is it about Alvin H. Butz, Inc. that appeals to the best in the construction management trade? "They have access. In a giant company, how often do you get to talk to the President? If a laborer has an issue and wants to talk to me, he can come in to talk to me. We try to operate so that if somebody has a problem they can come to me - just like if somebody in a family has a problem."

When you visit the Hamilton Street office building, you really do get to see the work of an All-Star team. It's functional art, featuring an exceptional use of space and natural light. Butz said the downtown office building was completed shortly before the evolving interest in "green" construction resulted in having established standards for Leadership in Energy and Environmental Design (LEED), the current standards by which energy efficient and ecologically thoughtful building are certified. However, in spite of not being certified, he is proud that the six story building includes most of the specifications. As a construction management company, Alvin H. Butz, Inc. has been recognized for being on the cutting edge of green-conscious construction.

"It has become a really big issue in the industry. A lot of 'buzz words' come and go. But, that one is not leaving. It's huge and it's another thing we've really embraced the last few years. We've been among the top fifty contractors in the country over the last few years in the volume of green construction we've done. LEED is the accreditation process - twenty of our employees are accredited and that's something we're excited about. Today, almost every project we're looking at is a "green" building or a LEED project. Especially the hospitals and colleges - they're all doing everything that way. A few years ago you were just starting to hear about it and now it's completely embraced by the construction industry." He says it's not just because the costs have come down on green technology and practices. "It's social consciousness. In a way, it started with the colleges - because a lot of college kids were saying we need this, it's something important, so they started doing it. Hospitals jumped on-board and it's just taken off. It's just unbelievable how the construction industry has completely

111

embraced it." As a construction management company, they are frequently involved in renovation projects where the costs of "going green" have been prohibitive. "It hasn't been done as much on the renovation side of things, but it's gotten a lot easier. A few years ago when it started out it was pretty expensive - much more expensive than normal construction. That's why maybe only the colleges and hospitals did it. But now it's a lot more 'user friendly' and the costs aren't as significant anymore to get the LEED certification. It's become a big thing."

To be ranked among the top construction management companies in the nation for their commitment to LEED Certified projects is in perfect alignment with the conscience of the company. In the same way, leading the movement for a revitalized downtown area, investing resources they didn't need to invest with the speculation that others will follow, is also what you might expect from a company like Alvin H. Butz. These decisions are in lock-step with the company's larger social consciousness. The record will show that there is hardly a local cause, significant charity, or non-profit organization that helps the community to which the Butz family doesn't offer some level of support. "It's critically important. Maybe even more to our family than to the company - it's really what I think our family is all about at this point. The Lehigh Valley has been good to us in terms of supporting our company, so we recognize that, and have done everything we can to give back to the community. Our employees have embraced it. They're on dozens of charitable boards and they're involved in Walks, Runs, and Golf Tournaments – everything you can imagine. We're proud that my grandfather's name is on a bunch of the buildings around the Lehigh Valley for the support we've given to a lot of the institutions.

"Our company has 100% employee contribution to the United Way for the last twenty years - every single person in the company has given to the United Way. My father ran the campaign, and I've been very involved in the (United Way's) Tocqueville Society. That's what we're all about. We've had a successful construction company, but at this point in my career, and in my father's career, our main thing is trying to give back to the community as much as we can. It's important. It's important for everybody to give back to the community. The Lehigh Valley does a great job of giving back to the community. We see this as crucial."

Greg Butz is a busy man. At the moment, the company is involved in renovation projects at Muhlenberg College and the Allentown School District, expansion and renovation of the Allentown Art Museum, new construction at Lehigh University and SteelStacks, and they have a few construction management projects beyond the Lehigh Valley. When he's not working, he is a perfect example of the adage that "To get something done, give it to a busy man." He is on the Board of Trustees of the Discovery Center and the President's Council at DeSales University. He also has a seat on the Lehigh Valley Hospital's Trust Committee, the Lehigh Valley Partnership, and the Lehigh University's Leadership Council. He gives, or has given, his time and energy to the United Way, Muhlenberg College, the Lehigh Valley Community Foundation, Easter Seals, the Minsi Trails Council of the

Boy Scouts of America, Good Shepherd Rehabilitation Hospital, the Boys and Girls Club of Allentown, the West End Youth Center . . . the list goes on and on. Is there any time when he just kicks back and relaxes? "I have a couple of boys that are playing lots of baseball, so I go to about sixty baseball games a summer. My father and I go to the games and talk to the boys and relax with that a little bit. I also play a lot of golf. So sometimes when it gets stressful here I disappear and within two shots I'm relaxed."

Of course, when the golf clubs are back in his bag, he leaves the links and returns to something he really loves. He clearly has a passion for erecting buildings that will stand for years to come. But there's something more. He sees his work as helping to build an extraordinary community. That is the work he loves - to develop the structures and tend the foundations that make the Lehigh Valley one of the greatest places on earth to live.

Maria Rodale

Rodale Inc.

The office from where Maria Rodale guides the nation's largest independent publishing house reflects a certain practicality. It isn't in any way austere, nor is it ostentatious. Instead, it's an appropriate size and adequately furnished to do her job. It is comfortable and functional. It looks like a busy place, sending the kind of message that you would respect as an employee, a vendor, a customer, or a visitor. In a way, the office of Rodale Inc.'s Chairman and CEO seems aligned with her understanding of the connectedness of things.

"When you have 'skin in the game' you work a little harder to figure it out. You learn a lot and what you learn is often different from what you thought going into it."

She is connected. To her grandfather and a legacy that has passed across three generations. To the mission she stewards, the business she directs, and the people whose lives she influences. Her experience, knowledge, intelligence, passions, obligations and ethics are also connected. These connections are woven into a fabric that

115

wraps around her activism, writing, being a wife, and motherhood - but, not necessarily in that order. In fact, she says family comes first.

You've never met anyone like her. On all fronts, she does serious work and faces unprecedented challenges. They are vast and complicated. Rodale Inc. employs nearly nine-hundred people who serve an industry that continues to change due to new competitive challenges and a shrinking base. That means survival in the long run, and the security of those who have committed their careers to the company, will demand the development of new products for the markets they serve, and/or even finding new markets. There is also the social mission of the company that pushes against a stone wall that is cemented together with mortar blended from a well-funded status quo, the scientific complexity of the issue, and the economic realities of the supermarket shelf price.

To promote an all-organic food supply might seem like a quixotic joust against windmills of big business. But, armed with proven research, she is hopeful that the weapon of reason will prevail. The business and the cause were well established before she was named the company's CEO. Both have seen growth and advancement for seventy years. So it's hard to imagine the pressure she could be feeling to add to the legacy. Factor into that pressure, an appropriate mathematical exponent because she became Chief Executive Officer during the most devastating economic crisis the world has scene since J.I. Rodale published his first word. Does she feel the burden? "Heck yeah," she laughs.

She doesn't carry the air of the stereotypical CEO. She has a two-sided business card saying she's the Chairman and CEO of Rodale Inc on the front and Blogger for Maria's Farm Country Kitchen on the back. She appears relaxed - fitting the expression "comfortable in her own skin." She can speak spontaneously about the things that interest her with depth and intelligence. She uses language that is fertile, rich and impossible to be misunderstood. She'll pause to ponder a question, not to consider what might make the most appealing sound bite, but to truly ponder it. That could explain why, in spite of the challenges the publishing industry has been facing, her company has done better than most.

"Clearly the biggest challenges are the fall-off in advertising throughout the whole industry caused by the recession; and adapting to new media, whether it's mobile phones, iPods, and websites," she says. "Definitely ninety-percent is recession focused. Maybe ten-percent is advertising that is coming back in different media and not coming back to the magazines." Like most comments she makes, she backs it with facts. "For instance, our on-line advertising is much more stable than our print advertising. However, you don't get the same rates. You make a lot less on-line than you do on the magazine." What is worth paying attention to are the Rodale Inc. successes that are not dependent upon advertising revenue, or put another way, someone else's success.

"For us, books are a huge part of our business. We're still selling books in a recession. Last year our book group had our best year ever." The book division posted revenue increases of 37%. This growth comes during recent years of dramatic declines in an industry that, according to The New York Times, has left major publishers with "a relentless string of layoffs and pay-freeze announcements" and a "clamping down on some of the business's most glittery and cozy traditions. " Last year, Rodale Books published twelve New York Times Bestsellers. Three truly stood out – each with enduring popularity that posted them on the list for over twenty weeks. Yet, such achievement does not suggest the future is assured without adaptation and change.

"We just went through strategic planning and have a lot of really cool ideas on new types of products, new types of ways of making money." She keeps a tight lid on the specific ideas; sharing little more other than it's a long range plan that sets specific actions to ensure Rodale Inc. will thrive in the changing marketplace. The statement reveals a CEO with the vision to know that defending who they are today with a market penetration strategy isn't enough to keep the enterprise healthy. "Part of what I need to do from a business perspective is transform this company from a publishing media company to a health and wellness company, so we're not just a magazine publisher, or a book publisher, or a website maker. Our mission is health and wellness and improving the environment. So whatever businesses help us achieve that are within our scope." To be accurate, this might be less of a transformation of the company than a return to the original mission of J.I. Rodale, Maria's grandfather. "From the very beginning it started from a health quest."

"He and his brother had an electrical engineering business." Maria Rodale explains. The brothers' decision to move to Pennsylvania wasn't driven by a desire to farm, to pioneer chemical free agriculture, or to start a movement. "They ended up moving out here because they got tax breaks to open up their factory. They were in Tribeca, before it was called Tribeca, in the Lower East Side. He came from a very unhealthy family. A lot of his brothers and sisters had died of heart attacks early and were really sick. So it actually started from the perspective of, 'How do I improve my health, how do I live longer.' So it was really a health mission. He started to think, 'Maybe there's a connection between how food is grown and how healthy I am." What he learned separated him from conventional thinking and few seemed interested in what he had to say. "He started *Organic Farming and Gardening* magazine first in 1942. He wrote *Pay Dirt* at the same time he started research, which began the Rodale Institute."

With the focus on human health and wellness, the magazine offerings have been broadened over the last seven decades to include *Prevention*, *Men's Health*, *Women's Health, Runner's World*, and *Bicycling* - a mainstream portfolio that appears on newsstands everywhere. The Rodale Institute, however, challenges accepted agricultural practices with substantial findings that are unpopular and regularly dismissed by . . . well, almost everybody.   We all know organic farming is probably good. But we also know that its prices have difficulty appealing to anyone with incomes less than the moderately affluent. Say the word "organic" with your eyes closed and you just might picture a teaming gaggle of Chukka boot wearing, "back to nature" misfits as its major proponents - folks, who without their 'cause,' might not fit in anywhere else. Or you might picture tie-dyed and sandaled vegans rolling out of a circa-1960's VW Mini-Bus, with peace signs and "save the earth" bumper stickers plastered across the tail. What you wouldn't picture is you. Rodale accepts this. "Here's what we know about changing culture. The facts come out before people ever admit to them. First comes the facts and then comes the opposition. And the opposition - because they know [the truth] - either have to create facts, buy facts, or ridicule. That's what happened to my grandfather." As the first organic farmer, J.I. Rodale was the target of derision. "He's a quack. He's crazy - the crunchy granola," she says, repeating the kind of campaigns that would discredit his work. She shakes her head as she considers what it might have been like for him. "The man never spent a day without a suit on. He was not 'crunchy granola.' He was a smart New Yorker." Since it's beginning, the work of the Rodale Institute (and others) has produced measurable progress. J.I. Rodale knew it would take time for the work he started to produce acceptance. He was patient.

"People have started to delve deeper. There's a great book called *The Secret War on Cancer* by a Dr. Devra Davis, and she writes about the history of the tobacco industry and cancer research. And both American and German scientists and doctors knew in 1930 that cigarettes caused cancer. When I had my first daughter in 1982, my hospital roommate smoked. In a hospital. It's unfathomable now. But the point I'm trying to make is we don't have seventy years anymore. We don't have seventy years." She sees the timing to be right for stepping up the campaign to share the latest research; challenge what she describes as misinformation; and expose the uncomfortable history between the government, the chemical producers, the education system, the food suppliers, and farmers. This spring she published her book, *Organic Manifesto,* documenting the connections between our health and the soil that grows our food. She dispels the myths behind why the greater population accepts chemical farming as a necessity, and outlines the steps necessary to ensure a healthier food chain and a cleaner environment. She says that the organic mission of the company is included in the long range strategic plan.

Asked how she balances the responsibilities to her company's growth with her activist spirit, she says "They feed off of each other. Doing the book helped me to understand where we needed to go with the business. Even on the nuts and bolts. Like developing a social media campaign for my book taught me things that a CEO without that personal vested interest in it wouldn't have learned. I might have said 'just hire some kids to do that.' When you have 'skin in the game' you work a little harder to figure it out. You learn a lot and what you learn is often different from what you thought going into it. So, I think they actually both work with each other." She suggests that her willingness to invest her "skin" helps her to manage better. It gives her the ground-level perspective that, consistent with her style, keeps her connected. "We work with a lot of authors, a lot of talented creative people. As a creative person myself, I'm able to understand, and appreciate, and respect what they do. And I think they may feel a little more comfortable coming here."

Maria Rodale was named Rodale Inc.'s Chairman of the Board in 2007. In September 2009 she assumed the CEO role. She laughs when it's suggested that growing up in a company would allow you to ascend to its Chief Executive position without any surprises. Then she pauses to ponder the careful explanation. "Anytime there's a shift in leadership there are surprises. There are things you thought you knew that you didn't know. Especially when you make a shift in an economic recession. I had a couple of years as Chairman where you deal with a lot more complicated financial stuff. But I also had 'on the ground' day-to-day stuff. Becoming CEO was like putting the meat between the bread. I was prepared probably more than most people, but there were a heck of a lot of surprises." Is there advice she can offer to others who might be promoted to a CEO position? "Never be afraid to keep asking questions until you get the answer. And then, be open to what that answer is." That's a strong departure from a management style that asks questions until the boss gets the answer that is most pleasing.

Among her earliest decisions as the Chairman was to improve the connections between the employees in the company. Rodale Inc.'s various departments include approximately five-hundred employees spread over three locations in the Lehigh Valley and over three-hundred in New York City. "I became Chairman three years ago and the first thing I did was start 'Lunches with the Chairman.' Let's pick ten people, five from New York and five from Emmaus and have lunch once a month and just talk. I went into it thinking there was going to be a New York-Emmaus thing - but there was actually more people from

New York that hadn't met each other because they worked on different floors. People from Emmaus had never met each other because they were in different buildings." Among the surprises she discovered during her early days as CEO were things she didn't know in terms of how people were getting along. "You think they are getting along and they're not. One of the things I do now, which has really helped, is I have a weekly executive team meeting. We have video conferencing - it's a little clunky - but we're all there no matter where we are. Sometimes I'm in New York. Sometimes I'm in Emmaus. It's the act of communication that makes it better as opposed to the location."

The company's headquarters occupies the original Emmaus office building. The company also owns a much nicer building on 10th street designed by Bill McDonough - a "green" building architect. "My mother insisted we [the Executive Team] stay in this building." There is an organic cafe in the headquarters that Rodale says isn't nearly as nice as the one on 10th Street. But, it offers over a half-dozen organic coffees, filtered waters, and organic food items. Is it an environment where you'd risk being ostracized for hiding Cheetos in your desk? "None of us are perfect. Nor do we strive to be. We're human. The essence of what we talk about is balance and moderation. Really, health is not a hardcore pursuit. We all know people who have done everything right and have gotten sick, and people who haven't done anything right and lived to be a hundred. So, it's really about trying to do the right thing more than the wrong thing."

The Rodale Inc. CEO admits being hungry for knowledge and current information. She is responsible for launching Rodale.com and finds great satisfaction in the information it delivers. The company does their best to monitor the effectiveness of the things they do to appeal to consumers. "One of the great things about the internet is that the feedback is instantaneous. When you put a magazine out on the newsstand it takes a couple of months for the returns to come back so you can read the results - and even then you don't know which cover line really sold. Was it the picture? Whereas on the website you can test every sentence and the click-through rates to know exactly what's driving people. To me, that's what's so exciting about the internet. It speeds up the knowledge."

As comfortable and natural as she seems in her role as the company's Chief Exec, it's still fair to wonder if there has ever been a time when Maria Rodale had considered another pursuit. "All the time," she smiles. "But everybody who is in a family business has to make a choice. Is this what they want to do or do they want to do something else? I actually made my choice early on. After I graduated from college I went to Washington DC and had a job working in socially progressive PR. I had this kind of epiphany where we were working on anti-nuclear, anti-apartheid, anti-whatever. I was like; I want to work on something that was 'for' something." Of all the things she might say, being "for" something is what separates her, and the company, from the typical activist noise that is heavy on emotion and light on pr4actical solutions. While the arguments presented in *Organic Manifesto* are strong in favor of all-organic farming and a chemical-free food chain, she is most definitely not anti-business, anti-government, or anti-corporate farming. She is not likely to rally a march on Washington that presents a "down with chemicals" front for the sensation of the evening news. Instead, she connects research to the problem, the culture, the economics, the history, and the potential solutions it presents. The research she offers in her manuscript has been tested, proven and then retested independently with the purpose of understanding a problem. There is plenty of blame to spread around, and as you read the book, you are not spared because of your political leaning, economic position, life philosophy, occupation, or dietary habits. The text discusses seventy-years of work, distilled into a workable manifesto for all of us. It's more than an urgent plea for something to be done. It includes action steps for government, farmers, business, economists, consumers, and activists.

Organic Manifesto is written with an engaging narrative voice and a meter that keeps the pages turning. In spite of the scientific talk, it is an easy read. And as astounding as some of the information is, there is great credibility. She delivers facts tied to footnotes, asks the hard questions that need asking, and reveals so much that you probably didn't know. It isn't preachy and almost - but not entirely - devoid of sensational language. Rodale connects the food we eat and the soil from which it was grown, to the rise in specific health issues. She connects the corn-fed beef bin at the local grocery store, the colleges that teach the latest "best practices" in agricultural science, the clubs like 4-H and Future Farmers of America, the farms that raise the cattle and grow the corn, with a snare made of money. Rodale's book describes a web of complicated entanglements that trap groups and subjects them to the will of companies that bio-engineer seeds and that produce chemicals that fertilize the land and protect fields from pests. She raises what are seemingly common sense questions that we may regularly overlook.

"Atrazine is a perfect example. It's the 'Number Two' herbicide in the United States. It's made by Syngenta, which is a Swiss company. It's banned in Switzerland." Not that being banned in Switzerland is reason enough to ban it here. "There was just an article in USA Today; literally almost every single well in the United States is poisoned with Atrazine - which leads to infertility. We all know people that have spent thousands and thousands of dollars on In Vitro Fertilization because they can't get pregnant. But then they go into the supermarket and don't want to spend $1.99 more for apples because they are organic." Because of the higher prices of organic foods, it might surprise taxpayers to know that chemical farmers qualify for government subsidies and organic farmers don't. In terms of input costs of organic agriculture, there is a trade off. Rodale says that the labor is higher for organic farming, but the cost of chemicals, fuel and other farming inputs is thirty-percent less. That's good news in her view. "Labor. It creates jobs. Organic farming creates jobs. So, it actually is more productive. It costs about the same. Shelf life has nothing to do with whether it is organic or chemical.

Rodale's book is 192 pages of information and anecdotes, plus a forward, index and footnotes. For the quick-read that it is, it includes tons of details. Tons of connections. Connections between the seeds, and their suppliers, and the rules regarding their use, study, and who actually owns them when they are planted in the ground. Connections between academic research institutes and the attachments to the money that funds them. Connections between the chemical manufacturers, lobbyists, and government officials. She details the conflicts between the Farm Bill (that limits the nation's agricultural production) and the reason there is a lack or regulation of the chemicals that are used in agriculture (so that there is enough food to feed the world). She explains chemical farming's damage to the soil, harm to the water tables, effects on wildlife and livestock, and its connections between the health of the soil and humans. She understands carbon sequestering, that bio-engineered seeds that resist weed killing chemicals increase the levels of poison in our water table. She knows empirically things that that most people passing laws regarding agricultural chemicals haven't a clue about or have little understanding of what they're causing. It's crazy, fringe, lunatic stuff . . . until you see how complete the evidence seemingly is, and even more so, the efforts to keep it suppressed.

What she writes is fascinating, if not life-changing. Rodale does believe in the integrity of the foods labeled 'organic,' which is distinctly separate from "all natural," "local," or anything else. "If it says organic it is certified by the US Department of Agriculture and there is a rigorous certification process it goes through. It's the one label you can trust." Her father, Robert Rodale, was responsible for getting the people together to establish the standards for organic certification. An automobile accident while in Russia took his life before the standards were implemented.

"Organic is really something that everybody should have a right to have. If you switched today to all-organic, you would see the amount of pesticides and chemicals in your urine be reduced by ninety percent in just days. Diabetes is caused by chemicals. Obesity, because it's endocrine interrupting. Autism, ADHD, cancer. There is a definitive link between childhood leukemia and a pesticide that homeowners and farmers use. Everybody wants to do a 5K to raise money for cancer. But nobody wants to just say, 'You know what. This is what's really causing it.' If enough of us band together and demand organic, the price will come down. We'll save money in healthcare and in taxes - because it's our tax money that's going to clean up all these messes everywhere or to pay for all this healthcare that we're creating by insisting on eating cheap food."

So how can organics be moved from the fringe to the mainstream? How can the perceptions regarding organic foods and the economic factors that drive the chemically produced products be changed? "That is a very important question, and it really is about uniting together. All the small groups. The fringe is a lot of little pieces. Most American's don't know what they're talking about. The vegans, the vegetarians, and the meat-eaters have to decide that they're going to get along. And the people who believe in probiotics have to get along with the people who won't eat dairy. This book is as much for those people - saying 'come on, if you're serious about changing the world you've got to get over your own self-importance, and your own narrow mission. For the sake of all of us, let's hold hands and create a broader movement." Does her being the messenger help bring all the factions together? "I hope so. I hope so. I don't know."

The company has a strong presence in the Lehigh Valley and Maria Rodale is connected. "I see a lot of really exciting things happening - some of which I can't talk about yet. I'm on the Board of the Lehigh Valley Hospital, and we've been talking about really doing some interesting things together with them - they're a very forward thinking hospital and we're a health and wellness company. There is a lot of interesting leadership here in the Lehigh Valley. I feel like in the last twenty years we've finally made the shift from being the industrial steel-headed community. Many years ago we had a professor from the Dardin Business School come in and lead a workshop with us. He said, 'You know, in the 1900's this was like the Silicon Valley of the day. Everybody came. It was the most vibrant place in the Country for industry. All the money was here. Business was cement. And where was it? The Lehigh Valley. Everything goes in waves and I think we're due for another wave. Less on the manufacturing and industry, and more on the cultural technology. Some of the best schools in the country are in Pennsylvania - and I want to bring those jobs here.

We are, and I have always been and will continue to be, committed to the local community. That's because we all live here and care about it. But also, because it is important to us in attracting people who want to move here and live here and work. From a political standpoint, what is interesting is our readers are both Republicans and Democrats. And there are extreme Republicans and extreme Democrats. And interestingly, Charlie Dent, for instance - pretty Republican - has been one of the biggest supporters of the Rodale Institute. Which is great. He's been great. Arlen Specter - same thing. Now he's Democrat - I was actually at his last Republican fundraiser. I personally am only just beginning to think about politics. When we put Obama on Men's Health, many people canceled. And I've written things in the past - I made a crack about George Bush when eating at a restaurant in Maine and people stopped reading my blog because of it. So, we're not a Republican company or a Democrat company. We're not a Green Party company or independent. We're for change. It's going to take all of us working together to make that change. And the same thing in the local community. It's not a competition. We're going to have to work it out. All of us."

While there could be a separate stories that feature Maria Rodale's life as a Chief Executive during transformational times and her life as an activist/author, there's an entirely separate story to be told about a woman who has mastered balancing a career with a rich family life. "Being a woman, there are not a lot of role models. There's Martha and Oprah - but they're celebrities, and they don't have families, and they don't have husbands. What's to me is exciting is creating a whole new model. I've got my team - my executive team at home. And I love them. My husband does work - he's a freelance copywriter. He's very involved in the community. He also helps out more than probably a lot of husbands. I trust him completely. If I travel I know the kids are going to be safe when I get home - which is really the important thing.

I've had the same babysitter for twenty-seven years - going on twenty-eight. She didn't always work for me but she's the same. The woman who does my laundry is in her eighties and has been working for me for twenty years. I've made my choice - my family comes first. And I learned very early on, that if I'm happy in what I'm doing and I'm fulfilled, then my family is happy. I don't ever want a jet or I don't ever want to have five houses. One house is good. If you have that perspective it's do-able."

That's the perspective she threads through all of her pursuits. It's a patient and savoring approach to living that recognizes that some things must happen now, but others might be better in time. For her, it's not a contest. "I think in terms of what can I do to further the mission of the company, the health of the planet, the health of people. I know when you study history, often people start out trying to do one thing and other things happen. I want to make progress. I want to see progress happen."

Dr. John Malloy, Ph.D.

Victaulic

Victaulic's Dr. John Malloy, Ph.D. is in an unusual situation . . . and it suits him. Forget the CEO icons of the 1980's and 1990's that became newsstand sensations by doing whatever imaginable to produce dramatic quarterly results, regardless of the unthinkable impact on families and communities.

"What's the biggest difference between working for a large public company and Victaulic? I pinch myself every day that I'm here."

Listening to the company's Chief, you hear a business philosophy based on patient wisdom and un-rationalized ethics that guide an operation striving to do what is most correct. This approach impacts the relationship between the company and its customers, those working in the company, and the communities where they have facilities.

From the helm of Victaulic, Dr. Malloy is able to steer the company in a style that is comfortably aligned with his personal ethics and also the moral compass of the owners of the privately-held, global manufacturer. When he first joined Victaulic, coming from the corporate culture of a publicly-held company, he recalls that the level to which the employees are valued came as a pleasant surprise. "The care and the concern that the owners of the company and the Board have for the employees is surprising." Genuine concern, expressed not in empty platitudes, but in tangible actions that few companies could justify because of the short-term impact on the profit and loss statement. "The pressures of Wall Street don't enable you to always treat every employee the way you'd like. [At Victaulic] every employee can get a second chance. Our Board, and our owners, would rather give up a little short-term profit if we could hang on to somebody that had the right skill set."

For example, when the economic crash hit the global business community, and Victaulic's business had fallen precipitously in November, the headline of the company newsletter said, "A Safe Harbor in the Storm." Dr. Malloy said he didn't promise the conditions wouldn't effect Victaulic, but the message was Victaulic was a safer than normal place for employees to see their families through the difficult times. "People will ask me, 'What's the biggest difference between working for a large public company and Victaulic . . . and I pinch myself every day that I'm here."

Among the obvious differences is how the Board wants to see the company ushered through the current recession. "There's not a meeting I go to now when we don't talk about who we've hired, how many sales people have we hired. We're hiring sales people now. We're hiring engineers now. Our business is down, but we're hiring.

They (the owners) just think this is the focus for the long term – the owners take very little money out of the company. They view this as a legacy their grandfather gave them. Their aspirations are to pass it on to their grandchildren."

Hiring to grow during a recession is unusual. Yet, the specific actions that were involved when the company needed to lay-off some of its factory workers last November would be unimaginable in most cultures. "Our business turned down, and our highest-cost facility is here. We anticipated that the first reaction of the folks in the factory might be that a temporary lay-off during hunting season would be tolerable."

Yet, Dr. Malloy explains, in today's reality, the company's contribution to their healthcare coverage can total over $1,000 per month. Such a financial strain could force these employees to make hard decisions about how they take care of themselves and their families. "The prospect of these good people not taking their medication, not getting their health care . . . we made a decision in an afternoon to just continue to pay their health care. It cost the company a couple-million dollars." There are places where making a decision like that could be your last decision, however at Victaulic it is what would be expected. "I heard from every board member saying we did the right thing. I couldn't have done that in a public company. And that's just a microcosm, there are many other examples. That creates a sense of passion and pride in the company. We did a management survey about two years ago . . . it was very revealing." Dr. Malloy says the survey asked employees if they were proud to work at Victaulic. "100% of the respondents said they were. Some good companies you might get 93% or 95%. That comes from our culture. The people come to work here badly wanting to see the company succeed."

The first impression one can get when trying to know more about Victaulic how easy it is to research and track the history and purpose of the company. Yet, information about the owners, and the backgrounds of its executive management team, is subdued. The low profile of the company's personalities, Dr. Malloy says is, "In part because the owners of the company prefer it that way. They're not flamboyant . . . In my case -I have to confess - it fits my personality. I haven't given many interviews." Granting interviews comes with some debate with his marketing and media relations people, especially if the topic focuses on him. "We did do something recently that turned out really well, frankly, which is one of the reasons I said, 'Well, maybe this works' . . . We did a piece in US Air magazine and got the attention of a lot of customers, and the employees got some pride, but the piece was about the company, so that worked . . ."

Staying well under the proverbial media "radar," there is one very interesting item that a Google search will uncover that bear's the signature of "John Malloy." Many companies have a Code of Conduct. At Victaulic, it clearly defines conflicts of interest, ethical decision making, and a variety of day-to-day issues regarding everything from the receipt of gifts and complimentary meals, stock ownership, and family-related business conflicts of interest. It contains procedures and processes to bring any infraction to the attention of management. "First and foremost, we expect that is going to guide us and change our behavior, particularly as we operate as a global company. That has become most useful in other countries of the world." He shares examples of behavior that might be acceptable in many cultures, yet with Victaulic's Code of Conduct would represent a conflict-of-interest. For example, he describes the foreign-based manager that established a business relationship with a family member that competed with a Victaulic customer. The Code of Conduct provided an avenue for the conduct to be reported, and defined the specific actions that would be taken to address the situation. "He was a good manager, but we had to let him go."

Victaulic's protection of company and the success of its employees and customers include other steps that are unusual for a privately-held company of its size. "We have an internal auditing department. I'm on the board of a private company, a little smaller than we are, and they don't have an internal audit department. And that comes back to a board that says, 'We don't expect to catch people running out the doors that are stealing. But we want to make sure there's a continual message from the board that there are good business practices." That's not all. "For a company our size, that has in the neighborhood of 3,500 employees, we have one of the large 'Big-4' public accounting firms audit our business. We are a privately held company and we have them doing our internal audit." Against the reality that ten of the top twenty-five major companies that failed in the most recent years were the result of ethical breaches and out-right corrupt business practices, this creates an effective firewall for temptation.

Dr. Malloy's career path and achievement over the years might have led him just about anywhere he'd choose to go. He graduated with honors with a B.A. in Economics from Boston College. He earned a PhD in Economics from Syracuse University and is a National Science Foundation Fellow. His career started as an Instructor of Economics at Hamilton College, a prestigious liberal arts school. In the early 1980's he spent two years in the Lehigh Valley with Air Products as an Energy Economist, after which he began a nineteen-year stint with United Technologies where he held a variety of positions including the role of President of Carrier North America, a $3.5 billion subsidiary.

Prior to being Victaulic's CEO, from 2002 to 2004, he was the company's President and Chief Operating Officer, and a Board Member. Yet, from where he came, Victaulic might not seem to be the most natural stepping stone for Dr. Malloy's personal advancement. You get a sense as he talks about his pre-Victaulic life, that he was looking for something more. "When I came I knew it was a good company, a neat product," Dr. Malloy recalls. But he says there was one key realization, in addition to the care for the employees that surprised him. "We are providing a product that has tremendous growth opportunity. It's cleaner, it's safer, it's easier for a changing workforce to use, and there's a marvelous growth opportunity. Victaulic is a growth company."

As Victaulic approaches its eighty-fifth anniversary, its activities have been as vital as a much younger enterprise. Since 1925 they have been an innovator in "piping system solutions." The grooved mechanical pipe coupling devices upon which the company was launched have a range of benefits over welded or braised joints. Developed during World War I as a way of adding speed to the construction of vital piping systems that delivered water and fuel for the Allied effort, it proved so effective that it earned the nick name, "Victory Joint." After the war, the company took its name from a combination of the words "victory" and "hydraulics." Today, their vitality is revealed in a range of progressive achievements.

The QuickVic Style 607 Coupling, won the Plumbing and Water Management category of Consulting-Specifying Engineer Magazine's "2009 Product of the Year" competition. This year they closed a strategic acquisition deal that brought AquaFlex USA, a leading provider of flexible connections for sprinkler heads, into the company's fold. Its Victaulic Vortex™ 1000 Fire Suppression System is now FM Approved as the World's first-ever Class 5580 Hybrid (water and inert gas) Fire Extinguishing System. It is so innovative, there was a completely new FM approval category established with a unique set of standards for the product. It was impressive enough to win the 2008 Product of the Year award presented by Plant Engineering Magazine. Ask Dr. Malloy how such vitality comes from an eighty-something, privately owned manufacturing company? "One sentence - and it sounds trite - but it comes back to the kind of people and it comes back to the culture. One of the most important things is the culture."

It's an interesting business in which Victaulic has established an ever advancing position. "There are two types of competition. We have the kind of competition that has followed us into the arena where we make a mechanical joint of the Victaulic style. It's called 'grooved.' That means we actually put a groove in the pipe and everything goes on that, whether it's a coupling, a fitting, or a valve. So we have some "grooved" competitors. But we capture a large share of the market and we earn a premium because we are selling a product that's typically a notch better - different technically, installs faster, and has a more reliable design. "And we're competing with what I charitably call fast followers. If you were to talk to really the only one or two western companies that we compete with, they have made a conscious decision to be a 'fast follower.' [They say], 'we're not going to have an R&D department to 'out R&D' Victaulic. We're going to differentiate ourselves by offering a broader line of products, or selling the Victaulic stuff along with some other part of the package in which we can develop some expertise.' So far we have been able to compete effectively.

"The biggest opportunity we have, the biggest competition is people that are welding or braising piping together that can still be convinced to buy the time and money story we have. You'll save about 50% of the labor. And you'll save 50% of the time. The time, very often, is bigger than the labor because if a contractor misses a date, the liquidated damages can be enormous." He jumps to examples where coupled joints can help ensure the best profit scenario. "Two of the best buildings for us to go after are casinos and stadiums. Because if you're not open on that opening day of football at 'the Linc' - which was a big Victaulic job - disaster. The liquidated damages are in the millions. "And Casinos. Even in low labor cost places, like China, people might say, 'I don't pay very much for my labor.' Yet, when they can get a customer in there on time - they can make up the money.

"Fifty-percent is a good bench mark [for time and manpower savings]. And then, how do we make money? The joints themselves cost more than a simple piece of metal. So you pay a little more for materials, but you make it up."

The company under Dr. Malloy's guidance continues as an innovative and vital entity, advancing the state-of-the-art in coupled joints, expanding through new product categories and strategic acquisitions, and constantly extending its world-wide reputation for leadership. When asked if there is any particular aspect of the company where he has left his fingerprint, his reply comes with little surprise.

"I know people who will say that what I brought three or four years ago was lean manufacturing or a lean philosophy, and we greatly improved our ability to deliver product on time . . . I'd like to think, you can only rest on that for a little while. So I'd like to think that more recently, we have a more collaborative management team. And we don't have any individual all-star. Not the people that work here, nor me. And I think the results we've gotten come from a team of people working together."

 John Malloy's Victaulic presents a strong example of the difference between squeezing the profit out of a market for in-the-moment results and the things that you do to protect the long-term future of an enterprise. Yet, it isn't simply that aspect of the company that gives him personal satisfaction. "On of the reasons I'm proud, is there's a great sense of social responsibility. Although the owners of the company don't live here, their view is we're part of the community." Dr. Malloy is careful to ensure the privacy of the owner's contributions to the specific charities, foundations, institutions and community causes.

Preferring that their names stay out of print, the owners epitomize the selfless spirit of charity and community involvement. Yet, for a company employing between 1,000 and 1,200 people in the Lehigh Valley, it is safe to say their generosity is significant. "In many, many ways, they take me to task to make sure we're moving in a way that's environmentally safe, and they have a view that we need to be a supportive part of the community." The spirit to do what's correct and be involved is not limited to the Allentown-Bethlehem-Easton area. "We're a global company. We have now five-hundred people working in Poland, four-hundred in China, and our customers are global. Employees are primarily manufacturing, but we have one-hundred to one-hundred-fifty selling and servicing Europe, the Middle East. We have about one-hundred in Asia now.

"About sixty-percent of our revenue is from the U.S. Forty-percent is not. We have an operation in North Carolina, and they have the same kind of [community involvement] effort. They want the people to support the local communities, the local charities. There's a sense of *noblesse oblige*." This sense extends to providing opportunity and growth for the people in the community. "Not only are we a large employer here, we're headquartered here. So we have an obligation. We have an on-going development program with Lafayette and Lehigh University. We recruit out of there." As Dr. Malloy looks forward to the needs of the Lehigh Valley, these kinds of programs not just help Victaulic, but also contribute to being better prepared for the future growth of the area.

"I think connected with this is the question of, what do we see happening in the next five years? And if you're apprehensive, as I am, about some of the trends that seem like they are going to happen, we try to look at the silver lining. "To the extent that New York and New Jersey become higher tax environments, it's probably going to promote growth in the Lehigh Valley . . ." Dr. Malloy says today the area is ". . . a good place to run a headquarters function and engineering function. It's a good place to recruit people.

"Victaulic recruits nationally, recently adding a treasurer and currently searching for an IT director and some other people." The quality of life in the Lehigh Valley is very appealing and helpful in attracting the best candidates. This hasn't always been the case. When Dr. Malloy describes his wife's reaction to his initial interest in returning to the Lehigh Valley, it might be a meaningful gauge to measure how far the area has come in the last two decades. "When I told my wife I wanted to take a look at this job she just went, 'hmm . . . .'" Her apprehension was obvious. "She knew what the Lehigh Valley used to look like. It's progressed a lot, especially in the last ten or twenty years."

Noting statistics that indicate the Lehigh Valley is among the top two metropolitan areas in the northeast for economic growth Dr. Malloy sees encouraging prospects in the year's ahead. "I would say cautiously that the Valley will do better than most areas . . . and that's because people are finding it to be a better place to live, to travel to work than other places. And that's because I think the neighboring states will become less advantageous."

In his comparatively short amount of time in the Lehigh Valley, Dr. Malloy has become engrained in its success. He is on the Board of Trustees for the Lehigh Valley Health Network. He resides on the Boards of the Lehigh Valley Economic Development Corporation and Valley Youth House. Between work and community, is there time for himself? "It's easy. I have a family. A wife I've been married to for twenty-eight years, a twenty-one year-old son and a nineteen year-old daughter. But, in addition to that, this is an easy place to make friends. It's a great community of people. I've lived in a number of different places and I find this to be a very vibrant area. In addition to family and friends, when I do want to spend time by myself, I go biking."

Spending time with Dr. Malloy, you start to understand how perfect he and Victaulic are for each other. He has found a place where his character and ethics are able to guide him. He has been able to focus on the horizon and cultivate a place where employees are proud to

143

contribute. He has many years left in his career, yet you can get a sense that he manages his day-to-day conduct with some consideration of the legacy when he does leave. "We have service award dinners at Victaulic. All of the companies I came from dispensed with service award dinners. And every year we have award dinners for the people that have been with the company for thirty or thirty-five years." He says he pays attention to how these people are remembered and that has given him the cause to reflect on how people may remember him.

"I'd like to be remembered as someone who treated everybody with the same amount of dignity and respect – beyond sales quotas and beyond achieving budget. In my position, if I can be approachable and people can say 'he always treated people with dignity' – I'd rather be remembered for that than anything.

"I talk about those who retire after thirty years, and think about their legacy. They might have been VP of Manufacturing or CFO. But it really depends upon how they treated people in the course of their career. Because that's what people really remember. 'What was the last thing he said to me?' or 'Remember the time you embarrassed me in front of all those people?' I've had this conversation with a couple of my colleagues – you can never take back a moment. You have to be very aware of what a stray comment or a stray criticism might sound like from someone in your position to someone in the hallway. If you forget somebody's name or you don't say hello to them, you can't go back and say you're sorry. You can't go back and make it right."

"Make it right." Those are perfect words to describe the ambition of Dr. John Malloy, Ph.D. One could hear it as an entreaty of uncommon purity in the corporate culture of America that has seen greed and short-term irresponsibility push the country to the brink of economic undoing. He operates as the caretaker of an eighty-four year old institution that seemingly exists to benefit the community. The owners could have "cashed out" long ago and allowed Victaulic to be consumed by the modern corporate mentality that strip-mines profit and leaves little left from the founder's original vision. Instead, the company seemingly exists to grow so that it will quietly contribute to the quality of a community. As such, for the Lehigh Valley, Victaulic is, and will continue under careful direction to be a rare treasure.

Dr. Elliot Sussman, M.D

Lehigh Valley Health Network

Dr. Elliot Sussman is an engaging personality. He carries himself with a quiet confidence and the kind of joy that comes from knowing he's been part of something good. He speaks in language worth savoring. No need for hyperbole. His smile is all he needs to punctuate a soft-spoken discussion of his work, his community, his family, and a good restaurant. He loves them all.

Dodging questions intended to evoke any boasting, listening to Dr. Sussman's version of his last sixteen years at the head of the Lehigh Valley Health Network, you could get the impression that he was simply lucky enough to be in the right place at the right

"Nothing beats it when you have young people around asking, 'Why are you doing it that way?' If the answer is 'we've always done it that way,' its time to retire."

time. The academic hospital's achievements under his direction are the obvious product of a sound growth strategy and an exceptional organization structure he should take credit for. Yet, he prefers to frame the institution's accomplishments with an all-inclusive "we," reserving words like "I" and "me" to describe his personal good fortune to be part of them.

He would never have predicted his history at the Allentown-based hospital. When he first arrived, he came to the Lehigh Valley after stints at the prestigious and traditional academic medical centers at University of Pennsylvania and University of Chicago. Prepared with Ivy League credentials that include a medical degree from Harvard and an MBA from Wharton, those were the kind of established institutions he was preparing himself to ultimately run. "When I came, I never thought I'd be in the Valley for more than three to five years. I thought this would be a notch on my belt." Yet, he explains two key reasons for his tenure leading the Lehigh Valley Health Network.

First, "It was just so much fun." Secondly, "In so many ways, we are at least the equivalent of those places in terms of caring for patients and caring for the community." He says that, given the people he worked with and the quality of the community, he could never come up with any reason why he would want to leave. Although Dr. Sussman is credited by many observers to have turned the hospital around, he rejects such suggestions. "I wouldn't take credit for it. I think LVHN has a fortunate culture. Its very large organization – we're the largest employer in the Lehigh Valley – and it's very complicated." He mentions statistics that say a complexity factor of "ten" has been assigned to hospitals. That means that the complexity of managing a hospital or health care organization with 9,500 employees is the equivalent of directing some other industrial organization with 95,000. This environment demands having people that are motivated and well-trained - the kind of people he hints were here when he arrived.

"I think we - and let me underline that "we" three times - didn't have to turn it around because there was already a strong organization. But we've made it. And 'we' has been the community volunteers, doctors, nurses, therapists, and our philanthropic supporters." He draws a parallel between the growth of the hospital and the growth of the hospital's employees. "We do things like our Institute for Physician Leadership and the Venturer Program." He describes a recent all-day retreat. "Three-hundred-eighty-five of us learning together for the day – in this case – on the Toyota Production System."

What does the Toyota Production System have to do with heathcare and hospital management? It shares many of the elements of the "upside-down pyramid" that Dr. Sussman refers to when he describes LVHN's organizational structure. He says, certainly, the CEO is at the top of the organization chart in terms of responsibility. Yet, in practice he really is at the bottom. "The CEO exists, as do the managers in the structure, to enable the folks doing work and to see that they have the right resources and training to do it." Naturally, in the same way Toyota has become a recognized model of organizations and business processes, by empowering those that do the work, LVNH's stature in the global community has made it a facility that has received over one-hundred visits from medical professionals from around the world. "People come in here and they say 'Gosh, this is a place that just feels different.' Healthcare is really tough. Lots of places you walk in and you see people walking with their heads down. Here they have a bounce in their step, 'Can I help you?' People really appreciate being a part of this organization. And having been here, and had a contribution to growing that culture, is something I feel really good about."

While the culture and empowering management style has resulted in LVHN being named on the U.S. News and World Report's list of top American hospitals for the last fourteen years, Dr. Sussman has other measurements that mean just as much. "I'd say were are at least as delighted, if not more delighted, by the fact that now, for three years in a row, we're one of the Fortune 100 Best Companies to Work for in the United States. Not just in Pennsylvania. Not just health care organizations. But in fact, that group of everybody across the entire United States. That's all kind of wonderful.

"Frankly it's the amalgamation of factors, that kind of recognition . . . I serve as Chairman of what's called the AAMC, the Association of American Medical Colleges. That's an organization that represents all of the med schools in the United States and all of the major teaching hospitals - and you know that's not about Elliot Sussman. It's about Lehigh Valley Health Network. And that's kind of a nice thing for all of us." Dr. Sussman shares a story about the time the hospital "re-uped" with the national insurance giant, Aetna. "The head physician who was down for the signing was asked by the local media, 'You didn't have this contract and now you're back here. Why is that?' "The Aetna representative said, 'Well, you may not understand this, but we have different sources of information, our own anecdotal studies, and our own resources. And there's public information. If you look at all of those, it's hard not to say Lehigh Valley Health Network, isn't among the top seven, at most ten hospitals in the entire United States. How could Aetna, a national insurer, not have a contract?" Dr. Sussman grins, "We'd pay for that endorsement. That was pretty nice to hear."

It's been over a decade-and-a-half since he took the reigns of LVHN. He still recalls two distinct impressions of his first day. "I looked at the place - and it was still a pretty big place, even though now we've pretty much doubled in size since then. There was a certain amount of both, frankly, excitement and fear. Probably, at that stage, there was more fear than there was excitement." He explains a career path in which he'd been fortunate to have reported directly to CEO's of model institutions. He had been exposed to a lot of talented senior managers. Yet, he had never actually been a CEO before. "It's different. It's different when it is all ultimately your responsibility." The other key impression of that first day came as he assessed the opportunity before him. "At the time, we were relatively little known. People knew there was a hospital here. But few saw the potential for what this organization could be with the enormously strong foundations that it had. I found it a little surprising that people didn't appreciate that."

"Sometimes, I guess one of my observations about the Lehigh Valley, is that it's a wonderful place to be, a wonderful place to live. That said, I think sometimes we have a little bit of an inferiority complex. It comes because we say, 'you know, its okay not to be the best, as long as you're okay, as long as you're good.' That's not what we're about, by any stretch. What we aspire to be is the premier academic community health network in the United States." When he says something as bold as that, it is delivered in a steady, matter-of-fact voice. He elaborates with a smile.

"I venture to say today, of the 125-plus medical schools in the United States, you could walk into any Dean's office and just say 'Lehigh Valley Health Network' and they'd say 'credible place.' And that should mean something, not just to people who work in this organization, but to the community." He chooses to use the word "credible" when, in our popular culture, words like "awesome" are assigned to achievement exponentially less significant. He aspires to be the best. "Credible" suggests there's much left to do. "We are in the midst of a biological revolution, a healthcare revolution. And we've known that for the last decade." The hospital looks for opportunities within this revolution. Dr. Sussman sees "a high likelihood that there will be very significant change in DC. We have been preparing for that for years and years." Some of that preparation includes having a plan that doesn't include him.

"Organizationally, for years we've spent significant resources in developing our people and planning for succession." Dr. Sussman understands it is the job of any good manager or any good leader is to plan for their replacement. Yet, he was a little surprised by how soon after taking the job that he was asked about his own. "It was my second day here and one of our former trustees, who used to be one of the senior executives at Air Products, bumped into me in the men's room. One of the things Air Products does extremely well is succession planning. That's one of the things they are known for, and if you look at the stability of that organization and its growth, I'd say that was a reason.

"My second day on the job, I'm washing my hands, and he walks by and says, 'By the way, done much thinking about succession planning?'. . . I looked in the mirror and said to myself, 'I didn't know I screwed up so badly." He laughs, but segues back to his point. There's too much at stake for everything to rest on one person. "They wanted a letter in a sealed envelope that only the Chairman of the Board and Chairman of the Development Committee would actually have an in-depth discussion about. They wanted a letter about, 'what if I weren't there.' The intent of that is that bad things happen." Unfortunately, it wouldn't be very long before tragedy would underscore the importance of such planning within his organization.

"A colleague of mine came here. One of the most gifted physicians ever." The way Dr. Sussman says his name you get a sense of the physician's exceptional contributions. "He was doing a phenomenal job in all kinds of respects . . . Then suddenly, he died while playing tennis on a Saturday afternoon. After that I set everyone around the table and said we owe it to this organization and to this community, to in fact, develop for each of us, a 'hit by the bus' letter." He instructed each member of his staff to write a letter about what should happen if they were hit by the proverbial bus and suddenly were no longer here.

It was suggested by a colleague that such a title for the letter was a little macabre. He suggested renaming it the 'Hit by the Lottery' letter. Dr. Sussman agreed, though he saw a flaw in the new name. "I told him 'if *you* win the lottery, I still expect you to show up here."

Throughout his career he always kept his hand in various aspects of medicine, health care, and community growth. From the clinical treatment of patients, the management and administrative duties of growing departments and institutions, the research that progresses the state of medicine, and educating the next generation of healers, he has had a measurable influence. He keeps a thoughtfully prepared schedule to ensure he is able to do more. "You can't do everything. One of the things we all learn is that you make choices in life. And sometimes you might wish you'd learned that a little bit sooner."

Dr. Sussman has achieved so much, yet you still get the sense that he sees himself as a work in progress. He invests a half-day, every second or third week, working with resident doctors at the hospital's community health center. Still able to make time for being at the bedside treating patients, and doing clinical work with students, reveals his passion for medicine and education. "That's good for my heart," he says. "Nothing beats it when you have young people around asking, 'Why are you doing it that way?' If the answer is 'we've always done it that way,' its time to retire." Dr. Sussman believes having students around is one of the ways you keep young and creative. He doesn't come out and say it, but you get a sense that the students teach him just as much as he teaches them. "I used to be a really good doctor. But, I'm five generations out in terms of what the newest and best. So much has changed."

Education is fundamentally important to Dr. Sussman. He has parlayed the reputation of LVHN into a twenty-year agreement with the University of South Florida in Tampa. In the arrangement, each institution will see fifty-six students, two-thirds of them from most likely to be from Pennsylvania, in a program in which their first two years are spent at the Tampa campus, and all of the clinical work of their third and fourth years will be at LVHN. "Plus, for us, this arrangement is not just about the medical school, but it's about USF health. That includes a school of medicine, a school of nursing, a school of pharmacy, a school of rehabilitation, and a school of public health. We've already been sending people there. They've been sending people here."

The value of being an academic medical institution can be profound in terms of quality health care. As a top teaching hospital, LVHN is at the cutting edge in an industry where the half-life of medical knowledge is estimated to be about five years. "So think about it. Let's say I was the smartest doctor in the world, I just graduated so I'm at the top of my game. If you're not keeping up in that area, in research and education, after two and a half years you'll know fifty-percent of what you knew, in another five years you know twenty-five percent. So in ten years you have gone from the smartest doctor in the world to maybe the dumbest."

The subject of community health weaves through almost every topic Dr. Sussman discusses. He links the imperative for economic growth and solid employment with the health of the community. "Growth and development - that's really important. If you look and ask, 'What makes for a healthy community? What's the single most important factor, in terms of traditional health rates – the development of cancer, diabetes, and suicide rates?' – The single most important thing is, actually, the employment rate.

"If you think about that, it makes a lot of sense. Jobs enable people to provide for themselves and their families. [Jobs] increase the likelihood of having health insurance. With health reform, that will further change." He says employment gives people a community to be a part of. It deals with their aspirations, provides opportunities for personal growth and development. In order to promote the health needs of the community, it shouldn't be a surprise that Dr. Sussman is on the board of the Lehigh Valley Economic Development Corporation. He was also the Chairman of last year's the United Way fund drive. He has a seat on the board of Lehigh Valley's PBS station, WLVT-TV, the Allentown Art Museum, and a handful of other community institutions, civic groups, and professional organizations. For Dr. Sussman, looking after the health of the community and the stability of LVHN doesn't start at the hospital's entrance.

"I grew up in Clifton, NJ - a town of 90,000 – not that different from

Allentown. My dad was very, very active. He was president of the local synagogue, Chairman of the Board of Health, and President of the Boys Club. Growing up, that was part of what you did. There was an expectation that what made great communities was for you to be involved in the community. "We're very involved in the community as a health care organization. But the health care community is determined in a lot of ways. One is to have great doctors, great nurses, great institution like this. But there are lots of other things that determine the health of a community. The health of the cultural institutions, its social organizations.

"So, there is also an expectation for all of our senior managers that they'll serve on the board of a community organization. I don't care which one. If you love music - how about the Allentown Symphony? If you like the visual arts - the art museum. You like kids - the Boys and Girls Club. That is also a part of broadening our horizons, and frankly giving back to this community. I find it, and most people do, really rewarding." If the health of our cultural institutions, the economic stability of a community, and the quality of its social organizations can predict the health if its people, what is Dr. Sussman's prognosis for the Lehigh Valley?

"I'm really optimistic about the Lehigh Valley overall. Clearly our nation has hit a pretty significant economic bump, and its going to take some additional difficult time and hardship, and we need to look at way to mitigate that and get through it. And that clearly affects the Lehigh Valley. "That said, I think we'll continue, if you look at the averages, to do better in terms of growth and in terms of development than the nation overall. This is such a desirable place. Many of the resources – the people we have here, the intellectual capital, the location, our institutions, our cultural life, and cultural scene.

"I remember coming here sixteen years ago and there were a handful of restaurants – now it's very different. I was vacationing up in Maine, I was able to call friends in restaurants here who would know this great place and that great place there, that are cutting edge, trendy and sort of like the places we have here.

"So, I'm optimistic. The Valley will continue to grow. We'll continue to see development of new small business. I think about some of the recent steps we've taken with the University of South Florida." Dr. Sussman hopes that could attract medical companies and health care related companies to the area. He sees an opportunity to further grow, and develop a small growing cluster of not so small companies like Olympus and B. Braun. "And I'd like to think, as we continue to grow and attract business, we may be able to encourage a few other medium-sized companies to ask, 'Why wouldn't we want our corporate headquarters to be the Lehigh Valley?'

He's not an imposing figure of a man, but his strengths are obvious. He's smarter than you. He keeps his knowledge-base as current as possible. You know he's ethical just because you couldn't imagine anything else. He's grateful for his good fortune. Don't expect Dr. Sussman to build buildings bearing his name as monuments to himself. Instead, he deflects the spotlight so it shines on every one of those employed at LVHN, all of the volunteers, and the citizens behind each generous gift that adds to the successful quest for improving the quality of health care in our community. He's not about gimmicks that post quick, short-term profits. He describes a long range vision to systematically expand, adapt, and adapt to the dynamics of the community and the state of health care. Dr. Sussman may have originally landed in the Lehigh valley to add a notch on his belt, yet he stayed and made something as permanent as permanent can be. Basking in glory comes to Dr. Sussman uneasily. The simplicity of how he relaxes is not very likely to come as a surprise. "Until about five weeks ago, I'd regularly exercise – I work out a little bit." He says today he walks and plays a little bit of tennis. "Less that he'd like. One of my vows is to play more tennis. I love to read, love the visual arts. That helps to explain my service to the Allentown Art Museum."

He has two children, a son and a daughter, who live in Boston and Palo Alta respectively. His son is an educator and will soon be starting a path to a post-grad education. His daughter is in med school. Neither choice could come as a surprise. When he tells you about his kids, there's a joy you can see he has in discovering them as young adults. From his expressions, there no doubt that nothing is more important to him. Perhaps, there is a close second. "I do love eating. [I love] being out with friends enjoying a meal at one of The Valley's great restaurants – and there are a whole bunch to choose from. Or at your own home. I mean, this time of year I just love sitting out in my garden and having a glass of wine at the end of the night. A little hummus or something else." He smiles, and talks as if making a note to himself. "I really have said I need to loose about six to eight pounds, and I think that's the lack of exercise. I need to start back. We'll get back to that."

Few CEO's across America, in any range of industries, could lay claim to the kind of recognition that Dr. Sussman regularly defers to others. His planning and management principles continue to set the path for systematic and sound growth. Initially, he never imagined being in the Lehigh Valley for any more than five years. Sixteen years later, he is the face of one of America's finest health care institutions, engrained in the careful management of our community, and by all measures, a tough act to follow. And how he wants to be remembered? "What I'd like it to be is, 'Boy it was great having him here. He helped make a difference in this organization, this community. Great guy, we wish him well."

While he hopes for nothing more than a smooth transition someday when he finally gives way to the successor he'd been planning for since his second day, Dr. Sussman says there is still much left for him and his colleagues to do. "One of the biggest flaws in the delivery of care is the cost. That's why we are implementing the Toyota lean concepts I spoke of earlier to become even more efficient and to reduce costs while maintaining the quality our community has come to expect."

He also believes that health care reform must provide coverage for all

Americans. "The culture of this organization is driven to make this community a better place. This is yet another opportunity to make a difference."

Tony Iannelli

Greater Lehigh Valley Chamber of Commerce

Tony Iannelli is an interesting study. Interesting and unlikely. The President and CEO of the Greater Lehigh Valley Chamber of Commerce wasn't specifically groomed for the job that he says on a scale from one-to-ten "is a fifty." Actually, if there was a search for an executive to lead the Chamber today, the internet technology attracting hundreds of applicants for every job and the "keyword" computer programs that cull the candidates into manageable lists, would very likely pass him over. He lacks a traditional four-year degree. His first job

"I'm pretty good at the whole delegation thing . . . You've got to allow [the staff] to shine and to make mistakes."

was putting tires on trucks at the Mack factory. Yet, 1997 when comparing resumes side-by-side for their practical experience, he had just enough of the right kind. "For a while I worked for the Economic Development Corporation in the City of Allentown, then ran the hotel for Ray Holland." He later managed the Downtown Improvement District and had a professional cleaning service that he ultimately sold.

With his experience in both public and private sectors, he was an attractive candidate. "Actually, I wasn't even their first choice," he says. "I happened to be really, really lucky." First choice or not, he was definitely the right choice.

The organization he oversees is far different from the one to which he was originally hired. It has grown dramatically. Today, as the times continue to change, so does his role. "I have to reinvent myself a little bit," Iannelli says. "The 'glad-hander' isn't going to work forever." His remark evokes a chuckle. Glad-hander is an epithet implying an empty suit, a practiced smile, and a contrived compliment - nothing of substance. The trail of achievement that reaches back for more than a decade betrays his self-description. Also, when he says he needs to reinvent himself, he should add the word "again." The successes he has brought to the Greater Lehigh Valley Chamber of Commerce have been the result of his ability to regularly adapt to the evolving, progressing dynamics of the area's business community. He reduces his success to one skill. "I'm good with people," he says.

He works at a tempo that will never short-change those who gave him their trust. It's a drive that has seen him achieve what those before him attempted without success - the consolidation of the independent Chambers from thirteen different communities to create a unified Lehigh Valley force. "People will ask, 'What was your plan? How did you bring thirteen Chambers together, take it from seven-hundred members to five-thousand and [achieve] all of the growth that we've had.' But I didn't have any [plan]." He gestures to his head. "I always said that there's a second person in there that's much smarter than the façade that everyone sees. *He* had a plan." However, when he explains the reasons why he may have been successful where others had not been, it is anything but random. Iannelli reveals a systematic approach derived from the kind of strategic thinking upon which all solid plans are designed. His ability to clearly see all the parts of a problem was fundamental to setting actions in motion with the highest probability for success. "What they kept trying to do (before 1997) is take the three major cities and bring them together as a Chamber." As a first step, the benefits of a consolidated Chamber in the eyes of the larger organizations in Easton and Bethlehem were not strong enough for them to relinquish autonomy to one based in Allentown. It would have been an uncertain step in an unproven direction. Instead, he was able to see a value that the Allentown-based organization could deliver to the separate and smaller community organizations. "We started partnering with the smaller communities because they didn't have staff and we could offer staff. So that's how it all evolved." The actions were focused - seeing needs of communities and providing a solution that they would find appealing.

"I think what helped is, that in this world, humility is a good thing. My approach had been, 'What can I do for you to make you happy and to serve you?' I would connect in a community with somebody - one, two, three, four, five people - and the rest would just work out. It's just so hard to describe. But the one skill that I had was perfectly aligned. We did it very pleasantly aggressive. I think that mirrors my personality. In some communities we 'golfed' them into submission. In some there was actual depth in the contract. In every case, once we got one started we brought the disciples with us. Once we sold the concept . . . we started with the Western Lehigh Group, then we went over the mountain to Southern Lehigh, then to East Penn, then to Greater Northern, Northampton Borough, then into Hellertown, then into Bethlehem . . . As soon as you joined you were 'in." The separate Chambers and Councils remained, for the most part, intact. Their leadership was incorporated into the management of the larger organization. There was clarity in the mission - the smaller organizations could go about their work on the local community level with the benefit of the 'critical mass' that came from being part of a larger regional force. "There was no closed society or secret handshake. So people believed in us and they knew that to the extent that we could, we would do everything to make them happy. It was that basic a principle. It just snowballed."

Each smaller Chamber or Council had its own identity, personality and style. The communities they served had their own unique qualities, priorities, and issues. "Once you start integrating staff, you do have cultures. And our culture was different than say what theirs was or Bethlehem's was. So we had some adjustments and some integration. Maybe not like a major company, but we certainly had cultures." Keeping the smaller organizations separate was the best way to serve the local businesses and to work with the municipalities. "In Allentown, Miriam Huertas grew up in Allentown and worked for PPL for twenty years. In Bethlehem Lynn Logue grew up in Bethlehem, her family owned a bar in downtown Bethlehem forever. Marta Gabriel grew up in Easton, that's her hometown. So we try to find someone that people can believe in, that's 'their person,' that they know loves their city. It's my job obviously not to alienate people or get in anybody's way." The achievements of the GLVCC have been aligned with growth and revitalization of the area over the last decade. The cities, towns, and boroughs have kept their identities, each contributing assets to give the Valley an identity much greater than the sum of its parts. "Our world is getting smaller. It's used to be very clear where Allentown started and stopped, and Bethlehem started and stopped. Now it's all one."

Because of the changes he has fostered from his first day in 1997 until now, Iannelli says the role of CEO for the Greater Lehigh Valley Chamber has evolved in three key ways. "Number one - trying to be all things to all people. Sometimes there are people, who know you that you don't know. With my personality that bothers me. Who am I to not remember them?" The second change in his role are the competent people that he has brought on board to add value for the membership. "We've got Michelle Young in Public Policy, who is outstanding. Marta Gabriel who runs our operation. Frank Facchiano runs member relations. We've got a great financial person (Dawn Wekheiser). Miriam [Huertas] in the City of Allentown. Lynn Logue in Bethlehem. Marta Gabriel in Easton. So, that's the neatest thing. We've grown from a staff of seven to twenty-five. I'm surrounded by all these really bright professionals, which I like." When adding new staff was there anything he had difficulty giving up? He laughs. "No. I'm pretty good at the whole delegation thing. I did it pretty quickly and pretty well. You've got to allow them to shine and to make mistakes. The point is we've got really good people and I love that. That's a blessing." Yet, the professional staff isn't the only thing that has grown. The work of the Chamber of Commerce includes "an incredible amount of volunteers." The number involved is daunting. "We've got a Board of fifty-five people, we've got an Executive Committee of thirteen people, and each one of the councils has its own Board. There is leadership - volunteer leadership, non-paid, volunteer community leaders out there that no one ever dreamed of, particularly in the smaller communities, who give their time because they care about their community. That's been another thing that's been neat to see."

The third key change is their focus on Public Policy. "We didn't have that when I got here. We have to promote a pro-business agenda. Last year was a tough year, so nobody was doing well. This year people are inching a little better." He said there is some concern that the Obama Administration, may not be familiar enough with the needs of business. "Do they understand that business needs to be profitable? Do they understand that business can drive this economy? I got to tell the President that when he came to the Workforce Investment Board. I said, 'Mr. President, if you don't mind if I could just mention one thing . . . Going forward, if you could just keep the profitability of business in mind with your legislative agenda.' I said, 'I don't want to give you the typical Chamber line,' and he said, "Well, that is the typical Chamber line.' But then he said 'I get you. We need to be mindful of it." To focus on the policy issues most important to the GLVCC membership is believed to be more critical now than ever. "The world changes at a very rapid pace, a very rapid pace and you have to stay ahead of that curve. We were positioned very well, and if we work with our legislative group, we can work together and get something done. If they know what our priorities are, we'll keep rolling." The force that the GLVCC can present to policy makers is much more influential than it would have been as separate Chambers. They can present a unified front representing five-thousand businesses and their 140-thousand employees that needs to be reckoned with by those who determine public policy at the local level, in Harrisburg, and Washington, DC. "We've got to deal with the transportation side, Route 22. That's going to be important. We've got to deal with the cities and make sure they get their piece of the pie. I think that's important. I think the airport is going to be important. I'm a Vice Chair for the Airport Board and that's going to be important going forward. We haven't used the airport to the best of our ability." The GLVCC's size in our "squeaky wheel gets the grease" legislative culture can resound in almost every lawmaking chamber where help can be found. Yet, there are some areas where the Valley can only expect to help itself. "The only losers maybe going forward are the cities, the urban cores. I think it's not a level playing field. They have less of a tax base than some of the suburban areas. Take Allentown, I think its like 35% of the buildings can't even be taxed. If they're an art museum, or City Hall, a post office. That number is unbelievable, and I probably am low. But at least 35% is un-taxable. Then of course the services are different than what you have in a suburban area. You have policing issues, fire issues, and public health issues they don't have. We started a foundation - we've already put almost $200 thousand in to the downtown, so definitely, we believe. We started the Greater Lehigh Valley Chamber of Commerce Foundation so we could drive money into the downtowns - so rather than cheerleading, we could actually put money into our partnering communities. We stepped up more than anybody as a regional organization. We have four locations, a location in every major city. I want us to be here. I want us to be in the city as opposed to the suburbs pretending we worry about the city. I love the cities we have here and I want to see them flourish."

When he speaks about anything, there is passion in his delivery. He can hold firm positions on a range of issues that somehow alienate few. Beyond being a likable "people person," Iannelli has proven to have the ability to look below the surface of an issue so that the solution delivers the best benefits to the most. If that's not something you learn in school, where do these qualities get cultivated? "I came from a big family so we were always picking on each other, you were aware of every fault. I went to Catholic school so I learned discipline and guilt all at the same time . . . We weren't handled with kid gloves. Nobody really cared how you felt. When you put the package together - it's like a lot of people from our generation - you think, 'how were we able to turn even reasonably normal.' Somehow we made it through." In such a training-ground little was given without being earned. He was cultivated in a crowded competition for attention and approval. From that he developed a restless ambition and a drive for continuous improvement and advancement. "If you tell me ten negative things about me I will remember them. You tell me something wonderful - that doesn't do very well. When you come from a big family, you're always competing, there's always a goal out there." As a result of his anxious drive, "I don't get to enjoy much of the successes because my brain is always going on to the next thing." He admits his schedule can be an almost full-time management job. "They kid that if Lorie [Reinert, the Assistant to the President] wasn't in my life I'd be in the parking lot with my Blackberry going in circles saying, 'I'm supposed to be somewhere, aren't I?'"

He is a man in demand. Golf outings, business openings, networking events, award ceremonies, and committee meetings all exhaust the hours of his day. In addition, Iannelli hosts a weekly television program. It's the place where his personality, his intelligence, and his love for the area are on display. "We try to make it different. We call it Business Matters, but we've done same sex marriage, we've done a lot of different interesting topics." As a host he might be best positioned somewhere between Bob Scheifer and Morton Downey. "We do point-counterpoint. I try to make it entertaining because everybody has a clicker today and they're going to watch you for about three minutes unless there's some sort of entertainment value. When I start the show I jokingly say, 'Please interrupt any time, and physical encounters are encouraged.' We've had some close to that." What Iannelli hopes to deliver to his viewers are local issues in an entertaining format borrowed from the national shows. "The perfect show is a good topic, point-counterpoint, a lot of contentious discussion - sometimes they get a little crazy and I've got to get a little aggressive in settling them down." He has created a program that reaches approximately two-million people and now is part of the media circuit for those promoting a new book or a political agenda. "We've had some biggies - we've had Hillary, we've had Newt Gingrich, and last week we had the former Governor, Tom Ridge."

As the face of the area's largest business organization for thirteen years, and a regular visitor to the area's living rooms through television, it's unlikely that there are more than a handful of personalities in the Lehigh Valley more recognizable than Tony Iannelli. He is among the few in the community who people expect to always be "on" and available. That has to build pressure in even the most affable person. So to decompress, he might escape on the golf course (but then, a lot of his link time is business related) or straddle the Harley that allows him a spontaneous escape - at least when the season is right and the weather cooperates. "But, there's nothing like the hockey," Iannelli says. He enjoys his ice hockey. Yet, he won't be found in the stands cheering. To escape the endless demands on his time, ideas, and energy, the Chamber CEO will head off to the one of the local ice rinks to be part of a game considered the fastest team sport on earth. You'll never see him sitting on the bench - his role is so important that he is in the game for every minute and found at the end of almost every goal. Actually, when things get a bit aggressive, you're sure to find him in the midst of every fight. "The moment that door closes and they start playing the music . . . that to me is the biggest, the greatest escape in the world." Iannelli doesn't play the game. In his skates, helmet, striped shirt and whistle, he is one of the area's premiere ice hockey referees. It's not a likely past-time for the Lehigh Valley's leading consensus builder. "I don't know how to explain it. I really like the kids. Particularly with the high school and college age - you can kid with them - they get it. The biggest compliment - kids will say, 'I love you Tony. You're the best.' As a ref, that really rejuvenates me." He was recently included among the nation's top Chamber of Commerce executives invited to Dubai to help the city understand how such organizations could help them. It was a week of being wined and dined, taken on tours, and entertained by a metropolis best known for its limitless wealth. "When I was going, one of the things on my mind was I was going to miss some of the playoffs. It was almost - Dubai or playoff games. It was almost a tough choice." He knows it's hard for most people to understand how officiating ice hockey could compete against such a once-in-a-lifetime experience. Yet, the intensity, the speed and the focus it requires to do the job well allows him to drop the Blackberry and block every other issue and pressure out of his mind. Being a hockey official allows him to be something and somebody completely different for a few hours each week. It's a great workout, skating up and down the ice at a pace dictated by high school and college-aged players. It has also made him a better manager. "The hockey thing was really helpful in my life. I have the tendency to want to be everything to everybody. It's good to be somewhere where I have to make really rapid decisions that might not make people happy and then have to stick to them." Of course, his personality lets the game torture him from time-to-time. "Don't think that if I make a bad decision I don't think about it at night. I can tell you calls I made ten years ago that I'd like to have back." There have been times when games were finished that Iannelli's greater nature took over and he converted back to the man so deeply concerned that he's doing the right thing for people. In the recent season he officiated a Bethlehem Blast game that needed to be won by the local team for them to advance to the play-offs. The goal that tied the game, and ruined the Blast team's chances to vie for the League Championship, came in the waning moments from a play in which every observer may not have agreed with the call. "What did I do the next day? I called Silvio." He placed a call to Silvio Martel, the team's coach and the Vice President of Hockey Operations for the Bethlehem Blast to express his regret that things didn't work out better. The referee knew how important the game was, not just the team, but to the entire Blast organization. "I think we got it right," he told the coach. Martel told him he was sure he did and added that his team put themselves in that situation by their mistakes at the other end of the ice. You could coach sports for a century and never get a call like that from an official. But then, most officials aren't Tony Iannelli.

If you dropped into the office of any Chamber of Commerce anywhere in the country you will find that they all really do the same thing. They may have varying success, but their mission is always to do what they can to support successful business. They introduce people to each other at mixers. They focus on adding value so that they can grow membership. They provide training and programs to help their members make more money. Behind the success are the people. There have been a lot of people involved in growing the Greater

Lehigh Valley Chamber of Commerce, yet nobody will argue what has been the driving force behind its transformation. Iannelli embraced the opportunity to the extent that the man and the position have become inseparable - and it isn't so clear whether he became the job or the job became him. Perhaps it was just meant to be - the perfect match that almost didn't happen. He admits his approach to work hasn't come without a personal cost. "I'm single. I got divorced when I got here . . . It was sort of good to get that out of the way because with the job demands, it would have happened anyway. And I've not remarried, probably because I'm married to my job." He says this in a way that assures you that, in the balance, he wouldn't trade his life for anyone's. "I meet a lot of beautiful, wonderful people so it's been a good run socially, professionally and so on. If something ever happens to me and you go to my funeral, I don't want you to feel a little bit sad, because this has been - for a non-educated local guy - unbelievable. It's almost indescribable what I've experienced since I've been here." That's a great summary of his leadership. "Almost indescribable." Better words couldn't be chosen to describe the man and his impact on the Chamber organization and the business community in the Lehigh Valley.

Tom Ridge

Former Pennsylvania Governor &
First Secretary of Homeland Security

When Tom Ridge speaks of his personal experiences with secondary screenings at airport security checkpoints, the image it congers is ironic. Why would he ever be pulled aside? Ridge is the most public face associated with the passenger screenings conducted at America's commercial airports. The Transportation Security Administration employees work for an agency Ridge created from scratch as part of his plan to keep the nation safe. His contribution to the safety and security of America has historical implications which will be recorded in text books for generations to come. As he talks you can imagine him standing with his feet shoulder-wide, arms extended, shoeless and unbelted, TSA agent with a metal-detecting paddle scanning him from head to toe. You'd assume that he'd be spared the inconvenience, but secondary screenings have happened to him over two dozen times. Ridge tells this story in order to frame a

"You can build systems, but people can't leave their common sense and their instincts in the parking lot."

174

more urgent discussion about risk management and personal freedom. He talks about the kinds of actions that have been taken to protect America while also discussing the more challenging responsibility of ensuring that the rights of Americans are not appreciably hindered. Homeland Security isn't just about protecting lives. From Ridge's remarks you can conclude that the ultimate job of Homeland Security is to allow Americans to exercise their liberties.

Beyond the horrific toll on life and the destruction of America's most symbolic structures the terrorist attack of 9/11 had an immediate and longer-lasting impact. It arrested the country's ability to move freely and comfortably, it slowed trade, it stunned the economy. Ridge was brought to the White House to return America to normalcy. He makes the point that we've always managed to be America in spite of such challenges. "Under [the Cold War] nuclear umbrella we built the strongest, most diversified economy in the history of the world. The Civil Rights Movement began and strengthened along the way. The technological revolution started. We put men on the moon. I mean, a lot of things happened. We accepted the reality of the threat and then went ahead and continued to build America." In his view, restoring America's ability to be America would be the result of prudent risk management. For example, it's not practical for every air traveler to be searched. So as a deterrent, the TSA will x-ray all bags, metal-detect all people, and then pull a few travelers randomly for a more complete screening. In his risk management philosophy, specific profiles matching the characteristics of America's known enemies should be given additional attention. He believes these are reasonable inconveniences to match the security needs of the day. More significantly, as he describes risk-management he makes it clear that intelligence must be interpreted, which creates a slippery slope to negotiate. At times the intelligence will present a clear need to act decisively. More often it is "fuzzy" and demanding a restrained response. "I'd be handed the Threat Matrix. Some days it would be a couple of pages. Some days it would be a couple dozen. They'd tell me the source - electronic, human, whatever - general description of the threat, etc." Ridge says, "If you believed all of them to be true, or all of them to be actionable, you'd never get out of bed." When he served as its leader, Ridge understood that the Homeland Security Department's activities would affect the country's peace-of-mind and any news that could suggest an elevated threat risk could return the country to its post 9/11 paralysis.

He talks about America's need to understand the real nature of our threats. One challenge in combating the enemy is the citizenry's resistance to accept the new paradigm of risk. "We tried something when I was Secretary. We to said people who travel frequently, 'Give me your iris, your hands, so I can confirm your identity. Give me your fingerprints so we could run them against the database. Give me some background information that your credit card companies probably have. And let us conclude in a risk-managed world that you're probably not a terrorist. Go through the metal detector. You can keep your shoes on. You can keep your computer in the case." He asks a question. "Why don't we do that? Why don't we have the political will to do it?" Ridge's question is born from understanding the best practices created in countries that successfully balance liberty and security against more dramatic and consistent threats than ours. He believes a practical approach to risk management is a principle that the country needs to accept in order for it to do the things that will keep it flourishing. "Let's accept the reality that another incident will occur. Are we going to put more and more money in security or are we going to put it into roads, schools, or other measures of defense? . . . You manage the risk. You continue to live your lives as they should be - as our founders wanted us to a couple hundred years ago. You don't compromise the way you live because of a threat."

There is a story told in his book, "The Test of Our Times, America Under Siege" (released in August 2009), that has led many to believe Ridge was once pressured to unsettle the nation's peace-of-mind for opportunistic political reasons. On the eve of Election Day 2004, intelligence regarding a threat to National Security was being debated by the White House staff. A popular interpretation of the conversation suggests Defense Secretary Donald Rumsfeld and Attorney General John Ashcroft argued that raising the threat level could help the GOP gain more votes in the morrow. That's not the story Ridge wanted to have gleaned from his printed words. "The challenge with how you interpreted the language in the book is one that I've had to deal with for quite some time. There was never ever, ever, any political pressure from any source to raise the threat level. There are those that interpret my remarks suggesting that somehow we were pressured. The bottom line was we were not. I did not want to raise it. [FBI] Director [Bob] Mueller did not want to raise it. A couple other

Cabinet members wanted to. But since there was no consensus we never did raise it." The specific quote in the book was related to the vigor of the argument which at the time prompted Ridge to wonder, "Is this about security or politics?" Ridge explains that the President created a group of Cabinet members who would regularly review, discuss, and recommend action from the intelligence being collected through the newly created information sharing system. Their biggest challenge was to determine what information was actionable, what was hyperbole and what needed deeper investigation. Disagreement would be natural. He explains that there was "rigorous debate" among the Cabinet members on the eve of the 2004 election. But he assures that it focused on actual intelligence that was gathered. "What Americans don't know is that group met more often and decided the intelligence isn't there, it's not clear enough, it's just not enough to put Americans on alert."

From Tom Ridge's history with the Bush Administration, you might have anticipated "rigorous debate" when he joined the Administration. Before being called to serve, his name had been considered for other jobs in the Bush White House. He was a potential Vice Presidential running mate. However, the overriding opinion was that the devoted Republican had personal planks that were not flush with the Party platform. He departs from the Republican core on key conservative issues like abortion, stem-cell research, and immigration. In spite of being the candidate recommended by Colin Powell (then the Secretary of State and once the country's highest ranking military leader) to lead the Department of Defense, Ridge was opposed by influential White

House insiders and withdrew his name. It didn't matter that he was a decorated volunteer combat soldier in Vietnam. His vote against the "Star Wars" defense system as a young Congressman tagged him with a record considered too soft on military issues. He was the Governor of Pennsylvania when called to join the Administration that refused him twice. It was a job he loved and that alone was enough reason to respectfully decline the President's request. However, his independence that might have made him a difficult fit for the Bush-Cheney White House was an appealing quality for a President who needed a plan against an enemy that was stealthy and capable of unimaginable atrocity. His independence would help him be successful as he built a network between twenty-two different Federal Agencies and their 180,000 employees. It would take uncommon skills to connect these twenty-two established bureaucracies and their fiefdoms, agendas, and distinct personalities. The country needed someone who could penetrate the Civil Servant culture with new urgency and changes in job descriptions. Because politics is the lifeblood and Homeland Security was the hottest issue in Washington, the Homeland Security Director needed to be someone who could succeed while large portions of his time were consumed by hearings scheduled by the eighty-seven Congressional Committees in the C-Span camera's focus which presided over a piece of his activities. Against all of these potential obstacles and conflicts the chance of success fell between slim and none. Yet, the urgency of the job was exponentially greater than the list of insurmountable tasks it included. Ridge loved being Governor, but this new brand of warfare brought the battlefield to his home and touched him very personally. President Bush was a "close friend" which also weighed heavily as a consideration. "I talked to the President that night and he generally outlined the idea he had in his mind. I knew then that the answer had to be 'yes.' The President said, 'I need a man like you, and you're the only *you* I know."

After taking the job Tom Ridge found an odd mix of resistance and cooperation from a range of fronts. He says Congress gave him uncommon courtesy. But he also became the lightning rod for criticism and ridicule. Late-night television and internet humorists found fuel for laughs. For example, telling homeowners to stock up on plastic sheeting and duct tape to resist a bio-chemical attack seemed, to many people, to be as practical as having school children duck under their desks for cover in the event of a nuclear attack. The color-coded alert system prompted a barrage of jokes and ridicule, including Martha Stewart fashion references and suggestions that his next career move would be to Crayola (where he'd have so many more colors to work with). There was political fallout. "A lot of my friends, Republican friends, said 'You're building a new bureaucracy - 180,000 people." It didn't matter that, "They were not 180,000 new people. Most of those people were previously employed by the Federal Government - all but maybe one percent of them." Ridge anticipated these kinds of challenges.

It's been reported that among Ridge's conflicts in the Administration was the nearest voice to the President's ear, Vice President Dick

Cheney. Ridge won't give credence to this supposition. "I'm just going to set the record straight. We now have a Nuclear Detection Office in the Department of Homeland Security because it was one of the Vice President's high priorities. He still fears, as most people do, that with the proliferation of nuclear weapons and nuclear material, we have to be worried. Maybe not so much immediately about a nuclear bomb, but a radiological bomb. The other area he worked is the biological threat. You take a look at what happened with H1N1. Did we have enough vaccines at the outset? No. Did they have the distribution system all set up? No. And that's when we had six months notice and we knew what we were dealing with. So the other thing the Vice President's Office helped us do - and where I wish Congress would be more active - is to build a much more focused bio-terrorism response capability. As three studies have confirmed over the last year . . . a more strategic threat, a more holistic threat is bio-terrorism. And Congress is still not paying a lot of attention to it." He recounts the culture of Washington and how the political environment is not always structured for solving problems. "The real challenge has been, how tough it was to get Congress - and it still is - to give up jurisdiction so they could be a true partner in building a Department. There were circumstances where I know some of the Agencies I dealt with went around us and went up to The Hill to get their way. Our way in leadership wasn't quite the way they intended. That was a disappointment, but it wasn't a surprise." Ridge realizes he had it better than most because of the grave nature of the task. He reflects, "If Congress, Republicans and Democrats alike, treated all Cabinet

Secretaries as they treated me it would be a great place to start building more harmony in Washington. Both Republicans and Democrats, when I appeared on The Hill, were very respectful. We didn't always agree. But we had good conversations. The kind of thing that is supposed to happen with give and take on The Hill."

"Good conversations" with "give and take" rarely characterize Capitol Hill debate, but they are the kinds of discussions that were regularly served at young Tom Ridge's family dinner table. He was nurtured by parents who were active in the political process. His mom was an involved Republican. His father a devoted Democrat. From his parents he learned to respect the value of disagreement and what is possible when there is dialog. He learned that neither Party had the franchise on all good ideas. Being conditioned to see all the angles of differing perspectives may have prepared him for success at a job where he needed to connect with people above the din of diatribe and posturing. There were new and nearly unimaginable threats focusing on America, and combating the enemy depended upon Ridge's ability to sell a new mentality to the influential agencies, policymakers and the general population. "I was, and I still am, surprised that the Cold War mindset of information flow was as deeply embedded as it was, even in the months and years after 9/11. The Cold War culture from the intelligence and law enforcement community was, and I think appropriately so, 'We'll tell you when you need to know. And we'll determine what you need to know . . . The 'Cold War Norm' was an umbrella of nuclear missiles pointed at each other. That was a reality. Now the 'New Norm,' or the additional norm, is what people call 'the asymmetric threat.' Now it comes in many forms. Terrorism comes from a wide range of organizations. So we had to divine a system . . . Primarily the responsibility is in Washington, but candidly you have to have engaged Governors and big city Mayors and police chiefs because we're not the battlefield." The well-established Cold War mindset promoted tight protection of information and broad separations of each Federal Agency. "We had a slightly different view of that. Our view was, 'We need to know everything you know. And from time-to-time, not only do we need to know, we need to share.' You put [information] in a common pool so that everybody in the intelligence community could look at it. Maybe the FBI has something that ties up with something the CIA has and maybe DoD picked up something on the battlefield." Creating the spirit of cooperation between agencies was the first step, but there was a learning curve that separated the will to do what was needed, and the culture to get it done. "Bob Mueller, who was a great public servant, briefed the President on something involving Homeland Security - a domestic problem that I was unaware of. I didn't know a darned thing. So afterward I said, "Bob what's going on?' At that point in time he said, 'Obviously there's a huge gap in the system. You can send one of your folks over for my daily briefing so you're not blindsided again.' We made progress that way, all along the way, but wasn't handed to us."

Comparing the work being done today versus the work of his fledgling Department of Homeland Security, Ridge can look back with some appreciation for how hard achieving anything could have been had the higher sense of urgency after 9/11 not motivated cooperation. "I think the current state of our security - it's tough to say it's good after Fort Hood and after Christmas. But there, and the President's Report suggests it, I don't really believe it was a failure of the systems and the mechanisms we put in place under President Bush . . . I think these are two classic examples where there was an error in judgment. It suggests to me that people aren't quite as vigilant or have the same sense of urgency they might have had if those revelations would have occurred a year or two after 9/11." He wonders with the information that was available, how the two failed terrorists got so far. "In Fort Hood, you've got an active duty Major having a stream of emails to a known radical cleric. We knew. We watched him when he was in Northern Virginia. Why that didn't cause the Army to do something other than give him a perfunctory review and let him move on, I don't know. They shared information, but they didn't do much with it. You can't design a system to make people use their common sense and judgment." While his voice and words remain steady and measured as he continues to speak of the recent breeches, his words reflect his ire. "The other one I think is an outrage. We have lamented for years that we do not have much human intelligence. We don't have anyone close to Bin Laden; we don't have that many people inside these terrorist organizations. A father, a reputable businessman, a known commodity, comes in to tell the State Department, 'I think my son has been radicalized. Oh by the way, I think he's been trained in Yemen'. . . Why at the State Department, on Day One, didn't they yank his visa and pick up the phone and say 'Put this guy on the no-fly list. If he has any concerns, have him talk to his father?' You can build systems, but people can't leave their common sense and their instincts in the parking lot . . . and in this instance, I think people just didn't use their common sense. We shouldn't be breathless about this threat, but those responsible for our safety and security have to be on their toes. And sometimes you have to take action and then ask for forgiveness later. If we yanked this guy's visa and we turned out to be wrong - too bad. You've got to err on the side of preparedness. And I think that's where we were let down. Not willfully. But it's a lack of urgency and we've got to rekindle that. I suspect this last incident has."

He also feels strongly that in fighting these threats we can not compromise who we are. Care to debate whether or not closing Guantanamo is a good idea? He will lift the discussion to a solution he believes is befitting our national character. "I think the broader world community would conclude that America has every right to pick up [and] detain individuals we find on the battlefield, or individuals we thought had either killed, or were in the process of preparing or plotting to kill Americans or our Allies. But, until we finally decided through our own Supreme Court that they deserved some sort of due process, Guantanamo suggested that America was going to do something that most in the world wouldn't think that we'd ever do - just pick up people and throw them in some desolate place and leave them there forever. Our values are our brand. That's why the expectation for America to conduct its business consistent within our value system - whether we like it are not - is what the world expects." Preserving our values does not mean allowing those who attack us to wrap themselves in the Constitution. "[Enemy combatants] don't have the mindset of a criminal. They want to kill. They don't care if they get apprehended; they don't care if they die. And they're not citizens. So we'll give them fair due process, but not all the protections afforded by our Constitution. The President has made a commitment . . . I think even he missed the point. It wasn't Guantanamo that the world was concerned about. I think the world was saying, 'America, where's the due process?"

Tom Ridge says he is no longer interested in being a candidate for elected office. He compares his retirement from political office with the record of boxer Rocky Marciano. He's taken his hits, and like the champion pugilist, he persevered through every round of his career as a Congressman, a Governor, and ultimately the first Secretary of Homeland Security. Instead of politics, he is now a writer, public speaker, and founder of Ridge Global, a private entity that has created strategic alliances with a range of expert firms in order to offer enterprise risk management and infrastructure services to the energy, telecom, electrical distribution, industrial, and government sectors. The mission of Ridge Global is supported by a heavyweight roster including Four-Star Generals, former corporate security officers, and foreign policy experts. While it's a new chapter of his life, it is still the same man doing what he does best - bringing together talent to solve world-class problems. John Manley, Canada's former Deputy Prime Minister said, "As the Canadian counterpart to Tom Ridge following 9/11, I quickly learned that he was one of those rare political leaders who was all about action rather than talk. A patriot and a public servant to his core, Tom is a pragmatic and practical problem-solver, a man whose word could be counted on and who truly made his country safer." All about action. Pragmatic and practical. A man whose word is his bond. All qualities reflecting a keen and uncompromised value system. George Washington once said, "Labor to keep alive in your breast that little spark of celestial fire called conscience." Accolades like John Manley's prove such a fire burns consistently in the leadership of Tom Ridge.

Bring It All Home

There are several threads that weave and bind the moral fabric of these leaders. They are competitive and vigorous visionaries that take measured steps to produce sustainable outcomes that improve their companies, the quality of life of their employees, the industries where they do business and the communities where they employ a workforce. As they lead, they all share three basic qualities. They have vision and know where they need to go, where they can go and how they must get there. They know what is important and put their resources toward serving a clear mission without distraction or knee-jerk responses. They have strategic wisdom. They know how to view problems, evaluate the elements that contribute to creating the problem and then solve the problem by understanding the long-term outcomes of their actions.

Strategic wisdom is critical. Part of being strategically wise is to create the culture that allows employees to be excellent. They all are empowering. They all realize that there are people within their organizations who may have a better idea, a unique solution or know the way to new opportunity. They know their primary mission is to deliver a service and product that can create customer relationships – not just sales. They approach their businesses and organizations by filtering all of their decisions through all of the relevant planning issues of market standing, HR management, innovation, profitability and social responsibility.

These were not just stories about leaders who are engaged in their industries and constantly change to improve so they can stay ahead of the dynamic curve. These are leaders with missions that improve the quality of life in a place that may only thrive because of the greater character of the local population. Aside from the leadership qualities of those featured in this book are the collective ideals of so many others who give time and treasure to create the conditions for economic success. Dr. Gast at Lehigh University remarked that the enthusiasm and energy of the Alumni was unlike anything she ever saw at any of the other prestigious schools that marked the way of her career path. As Phil Mitman said, 'It's a regional approach" as he discussed the many who volunteer and connect to make things better. As a result, the Lehigh Valley is a great place for business, for families and for ambitious young professionals. It's a good story that may run forever.

3

www.ingramcontent.com/pod-product-compliance
Lightning Source LLC
Chambersburg PA
CBHW022056210326
41519CB00054B/510